RAISED BY WOLVES

RAISED BY WOLVES

Fifty Poets on Fifty Poems

A Graywolf Anthology

Graywolf Press

This publication is made possible, in part, by the voters of Minnesota through a Minnesota State Arts Board Operating Support grant, thanks to a legislative appropriation from the arts and cultural heritage fund. Significant support has also been provided by other generous contributions from foundations, corporations, and individuals. To these organizations and individuals we offer our heartfelt thanks.

Special funding for *Raised by Wolves* has been provided by Edwin C. Cohen, Michelle Keeley and Mark Flanagan, Jill and Chuck Koosmann, and Aimee and Manny Lagos.

Published by Graywolf Press
212 Third Avenue North, Suite 485
Minneapolis, Minnesota 55401

www.graywolfpress.org

Published in the United States of America
Printed in Canada

ISBN 978-1-64445-265-3   (limited cloth edition)
ISBN 978-1-64445-266-0   (paperback)
ISBN 978-1-64445-267-7   (ebook)

2 4 6 8 9 7 5 3 1
First Graywolf Printing, 2024

Library of Congress Control Number: 2023940129

Cover design: Kyle G. Hunter

Beware of the wolves. They've been raised by wolves.

—Dobby Gibson, "40 Fortunes" from *It Becomes You*

CONTENTS

xi Introduction by Carmen Giménez

3 "The Miracle" by Kaveh Akbar, *selected by Leah Naomi Green*

6 "Stray" by Elizabeth Alexander, *selected by Claire Schwartz*

8 "No More" by Mary Jo Bang, *selected by Nick Flynn*

11 "Accursed Questions, iv" by Catherine Barnett, *selected by Saskia Hamilton*

15 "Ceremonial" by Eduardo C. Corral, *selected by D. A. Powell*

18 "Manhattan Is a Lenape Word" by Natalie Diaz, *selected by Sally Wen Mao*

22 "Because There's Still a Sky, Junebug" by Tarfia Faizullah, *selected by Threa Almontaser*

25 "Saint Augustine" by Nick Flynn, *selected by Fred Marchant*

28 "Trace, in Unison" by Tess Gallagher, *selected by Katie Ford*

30 "Now" by Christopher Gilbert, *selected by Elizabeth Alexander*

33 "Interrogations at Noon" by Dana Gioia, *selected by Roy G. Guzmán*

35 "Too Bright to See" by Linda Gregg, *selected by Tracy K. Smith*

37 "Winter News" by John Haines, *selected by Dana Gioia*

39 "Faring" by Saskia Hamilton, *selected by Claudia Rankine*

43 "The Crowds Cheered as Gloom Galloped Away" by Matthea Harvey, *selected by Mary Jo Bang*

45   "Primrose for X" by Fanny Howe, *selected by Jeffrey Yang*

48   "To Live" by Ilya Kaminsky, *selected by Catherine Barnett*

50   "The moon rose over the bay. I had a lot of feelings."
       by Donika Kelly, *selected by Danez Smith*

52   "Inpatient" by Jane Kenyon, *selected by Tess Gallagher*

54   "In those days I know now words declaimed the wind"
       by Vénus Khoury-Ghata, translated from the French by
       Marilyn Hacker, *selected by Ilya Kaminsky*

56   "New Year's Eve at the Santa Fe Hotel, Fresno, California"
       by Larry Levis, *selected by Mai Der Vang*

59   "For Su Bingxian" by Liu Xiaobo, translated from the
       Chinese by Jeffrey Yang, *selected by Harryette Mullen*

63   "Vaporative" by Layli Long Soldier, *selected by*
       Erin Marie Lynch

72   "Anna May Wong Goes Viral" by Sally Wen Mao, *selected by*
       Matthea Harvey

75   from *Trimmings* by Harryette Mullen, *selected by Monica Youn*

77   "Sea Sonnet" by Alice Oswald, *selected by Mary Szybist*

79   "The Rat" by Don Paterson, *selected by Tom Sleigh*

81   "Parable" by Carl Phillips, *selected by Fanny Howe*

84   "Boonies" by D. A. Powell, *selected by Diane Seuss*

87   from *Don't Let Me Be Lonely* by Claudia Rankine, *selected by*
       Solmaz Sharif

89   "Cemetery" by Rainer Maria Rilke, translated from the
       French by A. Poulin, Jr., *selected by Mark Wunderlich*

91   "*Blue*" by Claire Schwartz, *selected by Kaveh Akbar*

93   "The Estuary" by Vijay Seshadri, *selected by Susan Stewart*

96   "I once fought the idea of the body as artifact," by Diane Seuss,
       selected by Erika L. Sánchez

99   from "Personal Effects" by Solmaz Sharif, *selected by*
       Layli Long Soldier

101 "Eternity" by Jason Shinder, *selected by Sophie Cabot Black*

103 "gay cancer" by Danez Smith, *selected by Carl Phillips*

105 "Bee on a Sill" by Tracy K. Smith, *selected by
       Courtney Faye Taylor*

107 "Vita" by William Stafford, *selected by Jim Moore*

109 "The Forest" by Susan Stewart, *selected by Jennifer Grotz*

112 "The Troubadours Etc." by Mary Szybist, *selected by
       Natalie Diaz*

115 "So far" by Courtney Faye Taylor, *selected by Malcolm Tariq*

117 "From an African Diary (1963)" by Tomas Tranströmer,
       translated from the Swedish by Robert Bly, *selected by
       Vijay Seshadri*

119 "January 1911" by Natasha Trethewey, *selected by Donika Kelly*

122 "After All Have Gone" by Mai Der Vang, *selected by
       Tarfia Faizullah*

124 "Making Love to Myself" by James L. White, *selected by
       Eduardo C. Corral*

127 "Lent" by Mark Wunderlich, *selected by Gretchen Marquette*

131 "Ongoing" by Jenny Xie, *selected by Kemi Alabi*

133 "Between Strangers" by Yi Lei, translated from the Chinese by
       Tracy K. Smith and Changtai Bi, *selected by Jenny Xie*

135 "Hangman's Tree" by Monica Youn, *selected by Stephanie Burt*

141 *About the Poets*

151 *About Graywolf Press*

INTRODUCTION

The role of independent presses in fostering vibrant spaces for poetry is incalculable. Over many decades, the most significant and striking works of poetry have developed thanks to the communion between poets and their editors at small houses who strive together to, as Natalie Diaz so aptly writes, "speak or sing love into an unreasonable world." As an emerging poet I regarded Graywolf Press as an invaluable touchstone and came to its books for the profound and ranging influences that shaped my nascent aesthetics. When I imagined I might someday write a book that could find its way onto the list, I dreamed of being alongside those poets who are to this day indelible forces in my literary pantheon. Becoming a Graywolf poet felt like entering a vital and ongoing conversation in twenty-first-century literature.

Graywolf was founded in 1974 by Scott Walker in Port Townsend, Washington, as a letterpress publisher of poetry books, chapbooks, and anthologies, expanding over time to publish fiction, nonfiction, and translation. Graywolf incorporated as a nonprofit organization in 1984, was led by Fiona McCrae from 1994 until 2022, and with generous support from local and national funders has become an integral part of Minnesota's extraordinary literary scene, alongside other independent publishers such as Coffee House Press and Milkweed Editions. Graywolf's independent and nonprofit status and our commitment to the discovery and energetic publication of twenty-first-century American and international literature allows us to take risks, developing books and promoting authors from around the world.

Publishing significant and influential volumes of poetry that span the full breadth of contemporary poetry across registers, aesthetics, and languages remains at the heart of Graywolf's mission. Although movements and genres are ephemeral, transitory, or temporarily perplexing, Graywolf has nimbly captured the zeitgeist of any given moment across five decades. The list reinvents itself and actively champions work and voices that don't always fit traditional notions of poetry to interrogate what "tradition" might mean. In every case, Graywolf poets bring an exquisite sound and touch to their work.

Over the past fifty years, Graywolf has published more than four hundred volumes of poetry by hundreds of poets. Our books and poets have received national and international awards, including the Pulitzer Prize, the National Book Award, the National Book Critics Circle Award, the Nobel Prize for Literature, and the Nobel Peace Prize. Our authors have confronted the urgencies of our time, becoming profound forces for giving voice to what too often goes unspoken. Claudia Rankine's *Citizen: An American Lyric*, published in 2014, is a groundbreaking and vital book that prompted dialogue on everyday racial violence and has expanded our conception of lyric possibility. Published in 2012, *June Fourth Elegies* by Nobel Peace Prize Laureate Liu Xiaobo brought a haunting series of remembrance of the Tiananmen Square protest and massacre to a global audience. *From From* by Monica Youn, published in 2023, offers a trenchant analysis of nationalism during a moment of increasing anti-Asian violence. Graywolf books are in conversation with global crises, police and state violence, inequities, atrocities at the border, Native dispossession, mental illness, military aggression, disability justice, poverty, and many more of the most pressing issues of our time.

Tess Gallagher, Christopher Gilbert, Linda Gregg, Jane Kenyon, William Stafford, and James L. White are represented in this anthology as poets significant to Graywolf's foundations. Tess Gallagher's *Instructions to the Double*, published in 1976, was the press's first full-length collection. Gallagher might be describing the life of a poet when she writes, "It's a dangerous mission. You / could die out there. You / could go on forever." In 1982, Graywolf published *The Salt Ecstasies* by James L. White, whose work became a major touchstone for a lineage of gay poets, including Mark Doty, Carl Phillips, and Eduardo C. Corral. And in 1984, Graywolf published the virtuosic *Across the Mutual Landscape* by Christopher Gilbert, whose sonically rich poems have influenced generations of Black poets, including Elizabeth Alexander and Roger Reeves.

Over Graywolf's life as a press, we witness generations of poets with stylistic and linguistic variance and acuity, revealing formal evolutions and revolutions about what a poem looks and sounds like. Layli Long Soldier's *WHEREAS* brilliantly reframes government documents through erasures, recastings, and visual poetics to highlight the continuing injustices against Native peoples. Courtney Faye Taylor's *Concentrate* mines ephemera and archives in a wrenching elegy for Latasha Harlins, gunned down after being falsely accused of shoplifting a bottle of orange juice at a Los Angeles market in 1991. Poets like Harryette Mullen and Matthea Harvey create unique formal and linguistic innovations in disruptive and sensual play. Others such as Mary Szybist and Carl Phillips adapt classical forms and poetics to contemporary notions of reverence and moral inquiry. Diane Seuss reinvents the sonnet form in her exhilarating *frank: sonnets* in order to ruminate and argue for her life's trajectory.

Every poem is a miracle of discovery. A poetry collection is an expression of vision, but in each poem we read, we find the layers of close readings of others' poetry. We might liken reading another's poems to the fundamental work a dancer performs when learning a new dance by watching someone else. The dancer follows the gestures closely, brings them into their body, then translates them into their particular physicality. In Graywolf poets we hear the historical echoes of influence: George Herbert, Wanda Coleman, Rainer Maria Rilke, Rita Dove, Aram Saroyan, Henri Michaux, John Milton, the Dark Noise Collective, Ntozake Shange, C.D. Wright, Joy Harjo, Adrienne Rich, Catullus, Emily Dickinson, and William Blake among the countless others. Graywolf's ancestry spans generations of poets.

Tracy K. Smith, former poet laureate of the United States, said, "Graywolf is in the business of books that will last. I'm honored to be one of their authors, and to be published alongside many of the writers who made me want to become a poet in the first place." For this anthology, Jeff Shotts, our executive editor and director of poetry, invited fifty Graywolf poets to select and write about poems they love by other Graywolf poets. *Raised by Wolves* celebrates connections and lineages across fifty poems and fifty brief and luminous essays about them. The selections and reflections reveal what poets read and we learn how different poets dig into their enchantment, their unsettling. These short essays are like ekphrastic poems, or odes, or elegies, or fan letters. Erika L. Sánchez takes a synesthetic joy in a poem by Diane Seuss. Donika Kelly describes learning the power and careful attention to the line and stanza break through Natasha Trethewey's epistolary poem "January 11." Mai Der Vang loses herself in a poem by Larry Levis and their shared hometown of Fresno. Matthea Harvey takes on Sally Wen Mao's futurist depiction of early film icon Anna May Wong. Claudia Rankine finds communion in Saskia Hamilton's attention to the quotidian, the kinship of a gimlet eye.

A poet's attraction to another's artistry can defy notions of lineage that value only forward motion, and can resist the essentialism sometimes imposed by reading another's aesthetics. Across cultures, traditions, languages, and generations, we are in conversation. Carl Phillips demonstrates this in his engagement with Danez Smith's poem "gay cancer" when he describes Smith's ingenious use of contradiction and his admiration for their sly sonnet-making, while tracing an important lineage of gay and Black poets.

Regardless of style and voice, each of these poets share a commitment to transporting their readers. All readers hold a personal archive of life-changing or art-changing works—poems that change how they see the world, that affirm their place in it, or that assert a breathtaking miracle in the compressed universe of a single poem. *Raised by Wolves* attempts to collect and distill such encounters: fifty poets, fifty poems, fifty years.

I have had the immense and rare gifts of both being a poet on the Graywolf list, and now of joining its brilliant staff as publisher and director at our fifty-year mark. There is still so much to discover, uncover, and unsettle in Graywolf's next fifty years. The beauty of

Graywolf is that willingness to challenge itself, the future of literature, and our collective imaginations, and our striving to serve writers, readers, and communities remains unabated. I have been a reader of Graywolf books since I was in college umpteen years ago. Like many of the poets in this volume, I remember where I was when some canonical poems cracked me open. I read Linda Gregg's *The Sacraments of Desire* late at night after bringing home a stack of books I had heard mentioned in a graduate class. In her work, I found the central potency of compression and longing. I first read G. E. Patterson's *Tug* on a beach in Provincetown. The book introduced me to the vast formal range possible in a poetry collection. I recognize the fifty poems featured in this anthology have combined in strange alchemy to form the poetry that we write. Together, we are a root system tangled weirdly in kinship, and this includes you, reading this.

Art never happens in a vacuum—it's an accrual of relentless interrogation of what it means to capture the "slant" Dickinson instructs us we require to get to truth, though truth itself is a shifting and elusive focus, so poetry in its elastic capacity opens new portals into truth telling.

While there are infinite ways of being, poetry also has the miraculous, paradoxical ability to remind us that within the infinitude we share common impulses and hungers. As Kemi Alabi writes in her reflection on Jenny Xie's "Ongoing," "I don't want poetry to order disorder. Most days, I want the mess of life on full display. Then there are days when I flail for poems like they're footholds in the abyss." In this anthology, we hope that the full display of life's mess is also its joyous, communal gift.

Carmen Giménez

RAISED BY WOLVES

Kaveh Akbar
from *Pilgrim Bell*

THE MIRACLE

Gabriel seizing the illiterate man, alone and fasting in a cave, and commanding READ, the man saying I can't, Gabriel squeezing him tighter, commanding READ, the man gasping I don't know how, Gabriel squeezing him so tight he couldn't breathe, squeezing out the air of protest, the air of doubt, crushing it out of his crushable human body, saying READ IN THE NAME OF YOUR LORD WHO CREATED YOU FROM A CLOT, and thus: literacy. Revelation.

It wasn't until Gabriel squeezed away what was empty in him that the Prophet could be filled with miracle. Imagine the emptiness in you, the vast cavities you have spent your life trying to fill—with fathers, mothers, lovers, language, drugs, money, art, praise—and imagine them gone. What's left? Whatever you aren't, which is what makes you—a house useful not because its floorboards or ceilings or walls, but because the empty space between them.

Gabriel isn't coming for you. If he did, would you call him Jibril, or Gabriel like you are here? Who is this even for?

One crisis at a time. Gabriel isn't coming for you. Cheese on a cracker, a bit of salty fish.

Somewhere a man is steering a robotic plane into murder. "Robot" from the Czech *robota*, meaning *forced labor*. Murder labor, forced. He never sees the bodies, which are implied by their absence. Like feathers on a paper bird.

Gabriel isn't coming for you. In the absence of cloud-parting, trumpet-blaring clarity, what? More living. More money, lazy sex. Mother, brother, lover. You travel and bring back silk scarves, a bag of chocolates for you-don't-know-who-yet. Someone will want them. Deliver them to an empty field. You fall asleep facing the freckle on your wrist.

Somewhere a woman presses a button that locks metal doors with people behind them. The locks are useful to her because there is an emptiness on the other side that holds the people's lives in place. She doesn't know the names of the people. Anonymity is an ancillary feature of the locks. "Ancillary," from the Latin *ancilla*, meaning *servant*. An emptiness to hold all their living.

You created from a clot: Gabriel isn't coming for you. You too full to eat. You too locked to door.

Too cruel to wonder.

Gabriel isn't coming. You too loved to love. Too speak to hear. Too wet to drink.

No Gabriel.

You too pride to weep. You too play to still. You too high to cum.

No. Gabriel won't be coming for you. Too fear to move. You too pebble to stone. Too saddle to horse. Too crime to pay. Gabriel, no. Not anymore. You too gone to save. Too bloodless to martyr. Too diamond to charcoal. Too nation to earth. You brute, cruel pebble. Gabriel. God of man. No. Cheese on a cracker. Mercy. Mercy.

Leah Naomi Green on Kaveh Akbar's "The Miracle"

Like many poems in Kaveh Akbar's *Pilgrim Bell*, "The Miracle" holds a holy space empty by surrounding it with words, then striking those words to reverberate, like a bell. Here Akbar depicts the archangel Gabriel (Jibril) granting literacy and revelation to Muhammad. Gabriel finds the man fasting, empty in an empty cave, and squeezes him. It is an act that requires Muhammad's emptiness, but the poem squeezes the hollow man until his emptiness collapses, until the illegible world— loud with anxiety and the demands of archangels—becomes legible, meaningful, lucid.

Likewise, Akbar's poem has more interest in transforming itself than in transcending. It wants to be *in* the world, "cheese on a cracker, a bit of salty fish," but it wants to be able to *read* the world, to metabolize the meaning of the cracker and the fish. It wants this kind of literacy so badly, so genuinely, that we can feel what neither the poem nor we understand ("a house useful not because its floorboards or ceilings or walls, but because the empty space between them"). And perhaps this is what I love most about Akbar's "The Miracle": it so genuinely wants to offer that literacy because it so genuinely needs it.

I have a friend who, as a novice monk, told a mentor that he looked forward to his free time, the moments of the monastic day in which he was not meditating. The mentor asked him, "Is that really when you are free?" Akbar's "The Miracle" offers the kind of freedom that comes from constraint, the freedom that poetry can afford an otherwise running, relentless human mind, freedom of the delineated prayer rug, the meditation cushion, the temple, cave, song, stanza, the freedom of literacy: of emptiness not filled but squeezed. A kind of mercy.

STRAY

On the beach, close to sunset, a dog runs
toward us fast, agitated, perhaps feral,
scrounging for anything he can eat.
We pull the children close and let him pass.

Is there such a thing as a stray child? Simon asks.
*Like if a mother had a child from her body
but then decided she wanted to be a different child's mother,
what would happen to that first child?*

The dog finds a satisfying scrap and calms.
The boys break free and leap from rock to rock.
I was a stray man before I met your mother,
you say, but they have run on and cannot hear you.

How fast they run on, past the dark pool
your voice makes, our arms which hold them back.
I was a stray man before I met you,
you say. This time you are speaking to me.

Claire Schwartz on Elizabeth Alexander's "Stray"

One Friday afternoon in graduate school, I was sitting with a friend outside our professor's office waiting for a meeting when we heard the muted shuffle of sneakers. We looked at each other and laughed, then said at once, "That is not Professor Alexander." We knew our teacher by the sounds that exceeded her: the clink of her charm bracelet, the clack of her high heels, the voices of the students and colleagues who sang her praises and recited her poems. In her presence, I thought often of the French word *le sillage*, literally *the wake*, which describes the scent of perfume lingering in the air after someone has left the room—how the enduring fact of their having been there transforms what follows.

Elizabeth Alexander's poem "Stray" might seem at first to describe a contained unit—a nuclear family enjoying time on the beach. There is a mother, a father, children. And there is a dog—"agitated, perhaps feral"—who inspires a question from one of the sons: *"Is there such a thing as a stray child?"* In the final stanza, the boys run fast like the dog at the poem's opening—"past the dark pool / your voice makes, our arms which hold them back." As with the perimeters charted by the structures of the parents' care, the poem, too, unfolds in a neat shape, over four quatrains—the family unit, tidily squared. But Alexander's lines do not make of the family a border to keep love in. Rather, it is the carefully rendered form that allows for the magic of the breach, lineation that makes the enjambment sing. Two people who have found each other have made, yes, new life, but they have also made space for the reverberating question and its unwieldy routes. What is forged inside the careful construction, then bounds worldward—not stray, but free.

Mary Jo Bang
from *Elegy*

NO MORE

Goodbye to forever now.
Hello to the empty present and.
Goodbye to the orchids woven
With something that looks like a seed weed.

Hello to the day
We looked out through
The juniper smudge
Burned to remember the moment.

The doctoring moment is over.
A sheaf of paper drops like lead
From the tree of the table it came from.
The eyes play tricks.

The quilt edge clasped in the hand
Goes on and on and on.
Rumination is this. You
A child, then a man, now a feather

Passing through a furious fire
Called time. The cone of some plant
From a place I don't know
In the high flames.

Rumination is and won't stop
With the stoppered bottle, the pills
On the floor, the broken plate
On the floor, the sleeping face

In the bassinette of your birth month,
The dog bite, the difficulty,
The stairwell of a three-flat
Of your sixth year, the flood

Of farthering off this all takes you
As thought and object become
What you are. My stoppered mind.
A voice, carried by machine,

Across a lifeless body. Across
A lacerating lapse in time.

Nick Flynn on Mary Jo Bang's "No More"

The poem "No More" comes early in Mary Jo Bang's *Elegy*, and it contains all the awful energy of the whole. Awful, for this is a book that chronicles the year following the death of her son—by overdose—and the way grief can take up residence inside us ("The eyes play tricks," "My stoppered mind"). There is, in grief, the fracturing of days, a mirroring of what has been broken. Bang captures this in her jagged syntax, her starts and stops—the first two lines end abruptly: "Goodbye to forever now. / Hello to the empty present and."—as if the thought could not complete itself, as if the attempt to write a poem had drifted into meaninglessness.

Her attention here is simultaneously precise and drifting—"The quilt edge clasped in the hand / Goes on and on and on," followed by the barest possible ars poetica ("Rumination is this."). The effect is of witnessing someone gasping, the poet returning to the familiar land of language but the words now skitter across the page. It is the waking nightmare of grief that whatever her attention lands upon is instantly transformed into the beloved—"A voice, carried by machine, / Across a lifeless body."

The poem (and the book as a whole) is measured by the way time warps and bends ("lacerating"), especially in moments of tragedy: "You / A child, then a man, now a feather // Passing through a furious fire / Called time." This is elegy written from no distance, like a eulogy to be read at a funeral, but the funeral goes on for a year. Time has not been given the chance to do its terrible repair. The wound is still fresh. The poems shimmer inside it.

———————————————

ACCURSED QUESTIONS, IV

I'm ready to try riddles, which apparently helped cure Henry VIII of
dangerous melancholy, but the only one I remember is What did the
zero say to the eight?

Nice belt could be the beginning of something and might for a few
moments cure my melancholy.

Life, too, is dangerous.

Even days are dangerous. I'm serious. The ones around here can climb
the apple tree and shake it to make the apples fall.

—

Sometimes my questions come out as if I were interrogating you,
which is not my aim. My sister, who has the same upbringing, asks her
questions gently.

My dog used to cock her head when I asked, You wanna go for a walk?
Now she is ash on my ex's shelf.

In *King Lear, nothing* is often the answer. In Augustine's *Confessions*,
thou is never far.

I don't think we're supposed to question God.

Into the Pacific crashed a plane years ago. They never found any piece
of one of my sister's daughters and so there's the hope we try not to
indulge that the girl is alive somewhere.

Is that you, I sometimes ask under my breath when I pass a beautiful child on the street, though of course she is no longer a child.

Is that you, I sometimes ask.

I am blue this morning. High winds again.

—

Get up, I tell myself, and then I say you need to sleep, look at you.

Should I lie on the floor here for ten minutes and sleep or storm ahead, some brief exhalations, these hands at the ends of these bent arms.

Tomorrow I'll go through the *when*'s and try to understand something more about time, which is at the heart of the sonnets, along with love.

—

There are places in the world where people never ask riddles except when someone has died.

To be riddled with is to be made full of holes.

—

Jean, in "Sanctuary," asks:

You   who I don't know   I don't know how to talk to you

—What is it like for you there?

—

More than any other speech act, a question creates an other.

What are days for?

Days are where we live, writes Larkin. But who dreamed up this experiment? Are we in it or are we conducting it?

In clown class I was funny exactly once, when I walked through an imaginary square made out of four hats placed on the floor saying awful awful awful awful.

—

The only way to manage all this not-knowing is to hope in my next life everything will be clear, just wait. In the meantime, let me spend mornings here at Malecon, on 97th and Amsterdam, bent over these pages.

What are you writing, the Bible? the waiter asks. Why are you always working?

—

The novelist ordered a second glass of wine before he'd finished his first, a third before he'd finished his second. Red wine. Big steak. Two kinds of potatoes. Quite beautiful crooked hands. But what was he saying about sentences? Leave out the *and* if you're in a hurry. Solitude, and misery, may be necessary for a certain kind of work. You have to feel it first and if you've felt it you can just write the thing without explaining anything about it.

We said goodbye. We kissed on both cheeks. The subway wasn't working at that hour so I ran until I ran out of breath or the late-night bus stopped. Which was it? Which will it be? Solitude, misery, love?

—

Here in the city we have buses that kneel.

There are two questions in Philip Larkin's "Days," a poem that touches three of the four sections of Catherine Barnett's "Accursed Questions"—"What are days for?" and "Where can we live but days?" Barnett feels close to Larkin's questions because they are so dangerous. The experts come running for us. When I first read her brilliantly inventive, various, moving sequence, I was wholly taken by the poem and its questions. But I was not knotted up by Larkin's questions of terror and melancholy outside of the context of his own poem. Not that mortality has ever been far from my mind, but the isolated questions about the purpose of days weren't a great wonder to me at the time. (Now I wonder why not.) They were close companions for her. She explains, "Sometimes my questions come out as if I were interrogating you, which is not my aim. My sister, who has had the same upbringing, asks her questions gently." She is anxious not to be misunderstood but to understand.

> Into the Pacific crashed a plane years ago. They never found any piece of one of my sister's daughters and so there's the hope we try not to indulge that the girl is alive somewhere.

> Is that you, I sometimes ask under my breath when I pass a beautiful child on the street, though of course she is no longer a child.

Now, facing mortality myself, I return to Barnett's amazing sequence for illumination and companionship as we move steadily through the shared days. What are they for? The silence—or is it a stillness?—at the center of this piece of writing is holy. It is not a question of belief or not, because a missing child will never leave your side.

CEREMONIAL

        Delirious,
touch-starved,
    I pinch a mole
        on my skin, pull it
off, like a bead—
    I pinch & pull until
        I am holding
a black rosary. Prayer
    will not cool
        my fever.
Prayer will not
    melt my belly fat,
        will not thin
my thighs.

        A copper-
faced man once
    called me beautiful.
        Stupid,
stupid man.
    I am obese. I am
        worthless.
I can still feel
    his thumb—
        warm,
burled—moving
    in my mouth.
        His thumbnail
a flake

of sugar
he would not
            allow me to swallow.
                        Desperate
for the sting of snow
            on my skin,
                        rosary
tight in my fist,
            I walk into
                        a closet, crawl
into a wedding dress.
                        Oh Lord,
here I am.

D. A. Powell on Eduardo C. Corral's "Ceremonial"

"Ceremonial" is the first poem in Eduardo C. Corral's book *Guillotine*, an entry point in a collection that interrogates entry points, borders, questions about the body and what kinds of bodies are affirmed/welcomed/celebrated in this country prone to a history of exclusions and persecutions based on body type, body weight, skin color, sexual orientation. Is the speaker beautiful? Is he holy? The poem asks the reader and God to be let in. "Oh Lord, / here I am."

The poem runs down the page in a symmetrical, rhythmic pattern, a kind of rosary to "cool / my fever." The short lines are full of sensual pleasure: "his thumb— / warm, / burled—moving / in my mouth." But that pleasure is countered by the touch-starved longing of rejection and the low self-esteem of praying away the speaker's own belly fat and picking at a mole on their skin. Will God or man find us worthy? It's a tough battle with perceptions. "He would not / allow me to swallow," we are told about a lover, and we are reminded that the ritual of redemption in Catholicism includes swallowing the body and blood of Christ.

In the parlance of queer studies, when one is hiding one's sexuality one is "in the closet." But Corral reverses that meaning by importing ritual, ceremony, and devotion into the intimate space of the closet, where the speaker dons a wedding dress and announces, "here I am." In all my fault, in all my imperfection, Corral seems to say, I am still ready and willing to enter into a holy marriage with a male figure addressed as "Lord." The body is not invincible, Corral admits. But what else is there, the poem seems to ask, except to give oneself fully to the devotion that transcends the flesh.

Natalie Diaz

from *Postcolonial Love Poem*

MANHATTAN IS A LENAPE WORD

It is December and we must be brave.

The ambulance's rose of light
blooming against the window.
Its single siren-cry: *Help me.*
A silk-red shadow unbolting like water
through the orchard of her thigh.

Her, come—in the green night, a lion.
I sleep her bees with my mouth of smoke,
dip honey with my hands stung sweet
on the darksome hive.
Out of the eater I eat. Meaning,
She is mine, colony.

The things I know aren't easy:
I'm the only Native American
on the 8th floor of this hotel or any,
looking out any window
of a turn-of-the-century building
in Manhattan.

Manhattan is a Lenape word.
Even a watch must be wound.
How can a century or a heart turn
if nobody asks, *Where have all
the Natives gone?*

If you are where you are, then where
are those who are not here? Not here.
Which is why in this city I have
many lovers. All my loves
are reparations loves.

What is loneliness if not unimaginable
light and measured in lumens—
an electric bill which must be paid,
a taxi cab floating across three lanes
with its lamp lit, gold in wanting.
At 2 a.m. everyone in New York City
is empty and asking for someone.

Again, the siren's same wide note:
Help me. Meaning, *I have a gift*
and it is my body, made two-handed
of gods and bronze.

She says, *You make me feel*
like lightning. I say, *I don't ever*
want to make you feel that white.
It's too late—I can't stop seeing
her bones. I'm counting the carpals,
metacarpals of her hand inside me.

One bone, the lunate bone, is named
for its crescent outline. Lunatus. Luna.
Some nights she rises like that in me,
like trouble—a slow luminous flux.

The streetlamp beckons the lonely
coyote wandering West 29th Street
by offering its long wrist of light.

The coyote answers by lifting its head
and crying stars.

Somewhere far from New York City,
an American drone finds then loves
a body—the radiant nectar it seeks
through great darkness—makes
a candle-hour of it, and burns
gently along it, like American touch,
an unbearable heat.

The siren song returns in me,
I sing it across her throat: *Am I*
what I love? Is this the glittering world
I've been begging for?

Sally Wen Mao on Natalie Diaz's "Manhattan Is a Lenape Word"

"Manhattan Is a Lenape Word" by Natalie Diaz opens with a collective challenge: "It is December and we must be brave." When I first read this poem, I was struck by the declaration, the near ecstasy of the *must* in this first line. Diaz urges her readers to unflinchingly examine the ways we are in danger: in our lives, our ignorance, our desires. The poem journeys from a hotel room in Manhattan (The Ace Hotel) to the street outside the window (ambulance and sirens) to the inside of a lover's body—its lumens and bones. In a moment of pure intimacy, the speaker declares, "*She is mine, colony.*" It's a direct address to this city where the speaker is "the only Native American / on the 8th floor of this hotel or any, / looking out any window / of a turn-of-the-century building / in Manhattan."

The *anyness* of this city is alarming, much like the alarms of the ambulance. When devoid of Native people, Manhattan is a colony, and colony threatens to take away everything the speaker holds dear, including the beloved. All loves, for the speaker, are "reparations loves"—a recovery of what's been lost and needs repatriation. Debt flits across the lines—loneliness, like "an electric bill which must be paid." No matter where the speaker goes—even soaring in the space of a poem—there's nowhere to escape the grips of a violent empire: "Somewhere far from New York City, / an American drone finds then loves / a body . . . / like American touch, / an unbearable heat." The duality of the lines—mechanical drone (camera) and biological drone (bee)—seeks the same violent heat. By the end of the poem, the speaker poses the question, "*Is this the glittering world / I've been begging for?*" The reader, transformed, cannot answer.

BECAUSE THERE'S STILL A SKY, JUNEBUG

I turn on the porchlight
so the insects *will* come,
so my skin that drank of you
can marvel at how
quickly it becomes enraged,
a luscious feast. I'm waiting
to hear myself crystallize
with revelation.
Who stands guard at rooms locked into tombs?
Who will dictate the order
in which we're consumed?
—I turn the light off,
but who taught me to stay quiet
when the power is down?
You're so sweet, men say to me,
but tonight, I want
no one. Tonight, a drone
in Yemen detonates and rends the sky,
and in my father's garden,
drone is a stingless bee unable
to make honey.
I crush the antennae, regard
the exoskeleton. Do we ever learn
that we're given weapons
to be vicious so we can be sweet?
I look up,
because there is still a sky, the junebug
that whirs across it, because
there is still a head-scarfed girl

who sucks the sugar
from a ginger candy
before she explodes—I look up,
and the sky still flints with so many stars. Above me.
Above you.

Threa Almontaser on Tarfia Faizullah's "Because There's Still a Sky, Junebug"

After reading Tarfia Faizullah's "Because There's Still a Sky, Junebug," my perception of the foreign and forgotten shifted. This is a space most do not feel comfortable in, but Faizullah writes about it with an attention that makes you feel nourished.

"You're so sweet," men say to the speaker, and that sweetness is again tasted late in the poem, "because / there is still a head-scarfed girl / who sucks the sugar / from a ginger candy / before she explodes." Sweetness and grief are married here. And yet, this isn't a grieving poem, but one of wonderment and conviction. Reality is never ignored, but instead given clarity, no matter how unpleasant.

This clear-sightedness can also be said of the junebug, who whirs above our heads even after "a drone / in Yemen detonates and rends the sky." Faizullah sits beside me in this ancestral meditation, where I learn with a full-to-bursting awareness that historical trauma isn't jumbled messily in my blood, it's fastened securely to it. The junebug doesn't envy my two slow hands, my fear of every shadow. She doesn't always think about her faith and the one who made her. She thinks that the wind is warm, the sky goes on forever, and still I refuse to fly.

When the speaker asks, "Who stands guard at rooms locked into tombs? / Who will dictate the order / in which we're consumed?" I also consider the questions: Who will defend the disappeared, the invaded, the violated? Who will bear witness to what we pass down, and what does it mean to return? "Do we ever learn / that we're given weapons / to be vicious so we can be sweet?" That cloying sweetness again. Faizullah's poem encourages us to express both the tragic and the poignant as one, to open our eyes and *look*.

SAINT AUGUSTINE

Saint Augustine preached humility &
the need to simply be on the ground.
Do you wish to rise? he asked. What
would he say of these words then, which,
after all, are meant to replace us? What
would he say of the way I go back, again
& again, to the burning house, the house
we've already escaped? These words—
so quick, the way they rise up, like sparks,
or smoke, a person could get lost in the sky
watching them, a person could lose track
of the important things. Spot quiz: What's
the opposite of standing before a house
on fire, trying to understand the flames,
& knowing you will never understand?
I want to enter into that moment my mother
strikes her first match, but I'm still asleep
upstairs. In the dream I'm walking through
the marsh, because only there, surrounded
by water, am I safe. Are your hands
the water? Are these words the flame?
The reeds are taller than I am, the mud
slows everything down. In some ways
I cannot imagine seeing you again, but here
I am, kneeling as in prayer at your bedside,
counting our breaths. What would stop me
from taking your hand then & placing it on my
chest? *O Lord, help me be pure, but not yet.*
Even as I write each word I am farther from

God—sometimes I just can't find it. If only I could
have the faith I hear coming from the radio,
the way it always knows I'm listening. One day
these years will be known as the space between
silence & enough. I still have trouble being alone
in either, which is why the radio is always on.
Do you wish to rise? Augustine asks. *Begin
by descending.*

Fred Marchant on Nick Flynn's "Saint Augustine"

"Saint Augustine," the last poem in Nick Flynn's *I Will Destroy You*, consists of a substantive block stanza. Most of its thirty-seven lines are of eight to ten syllables, and have an iambic feel to them. The formality of this poem, however casual, stands in contrast to other poems in the collection. Flynn tends to favor short-lined couplets and abundant white space. By contrast, this poem seems like a final summary of several hard-earned, but not very comforting clarities.

The poem has an intense inwardness, as the poet traces an array of shifting thoughts and feelings. The poem brings to mind various soliloquies in Shakespeare, particularly those of Hamlet. Think of the way the speaker notes how he returns again and again to a family trauma, the "burning house" of his childhood. Think too of the speaker's longing for reconnection with a mother who had set the house on fire and years later would take her own life. Though only hinted at in this poem, the collection overall also presents us with the long ripples of trauma in a speaker who knows he has harmed himself, and via his addictions, infidelities, and bewilderments, knows he has harmed those closest to him.

For all this, "Saint Augustine" does not end in tragedy. The after-effects of the tragic are felt everywhere, but the poet/speaker is a survivor. Yes, he keeps returning to wounds that cannot be healed. Yes, he wishes his questions had answers. However, this poem charts a journey into the many enigmas of human suffering. Line by line, we accompany this poet in a descent to the ground of his being, his pain, longing, and loneliness palpable at every step. That activity is, as Keats put it, the hard work we do in this "vale of soul-making." Maybe that labor is what Augustine meant by "descending." Maybe such soul-making is nearly synonymous with making poems like this.

TRACE, IN UNISON

Terrible, the rain. All night, rain
that I love. So the weight of his leg
falls again like a huge tender wing
across my hipbone. Its continuing—the rain,
as he does not. Except as that caress
most inhabited. Ellipsis of
eucalyptus. His arms, his beautiful
careless breathing. Inscription
contralto where his lips graze
the bow of my neck. Muslin half-light.
Musk of kerosene in the hall, fixative
to ceaselessly this rain, in which
there is nothing to do but be happy, be
free, as if someone sadly accused
came in with their coat soaked through
and said, "But I only wanted
to weep and love," and we rolled toward
the voice like one body and said
with our eyes closed, "Then weep, then
love." Buds of jasmine threaded through
her hair so they opened after dark,
brightening the room. That morning
rain as it would fall, still
falling, and where we had lain,
an arctic light steady
in the mind's releasing.

Katie Ford on Tess Gallagher's "Trace, in Unison"

In 1976, Graywolf published its first full-length book of poems, Tess Gallagher's *Instructions to the Double*. If "instructions" sounds like a trustworthy guide to the wilderness, "the double" multiplies the sense of who we are in the wilderness, and not just by any number, but by perhaps the most compelling, most complexifying number: two. *Two* is the way of the poet. *One* cannot create figuration, always another is needed: metaphor reveals two yet-undisclosed equivalencies; irony needs its sincere, unspoken counterpart to even have a name; and the impossibility at the core of paradox yearns to prove it belongs to what is called the possible world.

Gallagher is our great living poet of the leap, of crossing such chasms, of lines that are tracks laid down by her going-ahead-of-us into that internal and external *Is, Is Not*, that ultimate double that pains and revives and pains us again, standing together as the title of her most recent collection, words not undoing but devoting themselves to each other, spousal and ongoing. Luckily for us, it seems Gallagher was given not one but two imaginations at birth, that's how innate the unfurling feels. A simile, for her, is more like a quest than a likeness, and when she sets out in these ways, I often feel like I'm in the poem's small boat, and she is both gust and sail at once, and then when I turn to look, there she is, sitting beside me. Companioned and transformed, I arrive on the other side, having traveled a miniature distance of words the soul's metric deems enormous.

And so, when I need to remember what only a poem can do, I return to Gallagher's work, I say aloud the first two fragments of "Trace, in Unison," just as I have for the last twenty-five years, since I first heard her read them, and when I need to remember again, I know just where to go—"Terrible, the rain. All night, rain / that I love . . ."

NOW

I park the car because I'm happy,
because if everyone parked we'd have a street party,
because the moon is full—
it is orange, the sky is closer
and it would be wrong to drive into it.
This is the first day of summer—
everyone is hanging out,
women walk by in their bodies so mellow
I feel I'm near a friend's house.

The small white flakes of the headlights
sweat for a second on the storefronts.
In the windows, darkened afterhours,
a reflection stares back
looking more like me than me.
I reach to touch
and the reflection touches me.
Everything is perfect—
even my skin fits.

Hanging out,
the taillights of the turning cars
are fires, going out—
are the spaces of roses flowered
deeper in themselves. I close my eyes
and am flowered deeper in myself.
Further up the street a walking figure
I can't make out, a face
behind a bag of groceries, free arm swinging

in the air the wave of a deep red
fluid shifting to and fro.

At the vegetarian restaurant
I see it's Michael the Conga Drummer—
been looking for him 2 months.
He asks me, "What's happening."
I love his fingers.
When we shake hands I mix his grip
with the curve of my father's
toting cantelope in the house from the market.
We are two griots at an intersection.
I answer him in parable:
the orange that I've been carrying
is some luminous memory, bursting,
bigger than my hand can hold,
so I hand him half.

Elizabeth Alexander on Christopher Gilbert's "Now"

We are alive; we are together; it is the first day of summer. Christopher Gilbert's "Now" captures the simple beauty of hanging out. Being in community in this poem is more than an everyday hang, enabling the speaker to feel "flowered deeper in myself." He looks in a storefront window and "a reflection stares back / looking more like me than me." He feels that "Everything is perfect— / even my skin fits." To be comfortable in our own skin is to feel at home within ourselves, yes, and for the speaker, the threats that living in Black skin and being out in public can bring are, for an extended moment, not there. "Even" lets us know it surprises the speaker. But this is also a sustained moment of peace and joy that the poem lets us believe could last forever.

When the two friends meet, they dap each other up and in that theater of friendship the speaker finds a deeper connection, "I love his fingers. / When we shake hands I mix his grip / with the curve of my father's / toting cantelope in the house from the market." The handshake connects him to kin past and present. For indeed, after that handshake comes the declaration that stops us: "We are two griots at an intersection." And then, "I answer him in parable." After ritual touch the speaker has the ability to distill the wisdom of elders and generations into pith and meaning. A cantelope is bigger than an orange; the elder's hands span the bigger fruit, and in the handshake, the son aspires to the span and breadth of generational knowing.

So much beauty as this poem comes to the end on that orange, "some luminous memory, bursting, / bigger than my hand can hold." And then, the poem ends seemingly inevitably: "so I hand him half." In the face of such blossom and abundance, there is only one thing to do: connect and commune.

Dana Gioia

from *99 Poems: New & Selected*

INTERROGATIONS AT NOON

Just before noon I often hear a voice,
Cool and insistent, whispering in my head.
It is the better man I might have been,
Who chronicles the life I've never led.

He cannot understand what grim mistake
Granted me life but left him still unborn.
He views his wayward brother with regret
And hardly bothers to disguise his scorn.

"Who is the person you pretend to be?"
He asks, "The failed saint, the simpering bore,
The pale connoisseur of spent desire,
The half-hearted hermit eyeing the door?

"You cultivate confusion like a rose
In watery lies too weak to be untrue,
And play the minor figures in the pageant,
Extravagant and empty, that is you."

Roy G. Guzmán on Dana Gioia's "Interrogations at Noon"

I can picture the "better man I might have been"—from Dana Gioia's poem "Interrogations at Noon"—commiserating with the narrator of Jorge Luis Borges's "Borges and I." They exchange scathing gossip about their lesser selves—about the pages that might have been written, of promises left unhatched, or Gioia's "wayward brother" who, like Borges's vain "other one," alters life's stupendous simplicities into rootless mannerisms. Wasted energy. Uncommitted acts.

Whoever prompts this voice to deliver his damning verdict must have never agonized over employment opportunities. He hasn't just strolled through the streets of Borges's Buenos Aires, or taken peeks at Gioia's Los Angeles neighborhoods. He's the doorkeeper of Kafka's "Before the Law." The Freudian unconscious. Ebenezer Scrooge's ghosts. The Incredible Hulk.

Gioia's narrator vanishes under the weight of this voice's chastisement, which begins as a polycephalic question and culminates with a rebuke of the narrator's knack for breeding uncertainty and phoniness. By the end of the poem, a sour taste sets camp in my mouth: why should this voice have that much agency?

It is quite telling that, in *Interrogations at Noon*, Gioia's title poem sits between two striking epiphanies: a husband gazing at his wife as he realizes he is now a ghost in her life, and a parent's proud meditation on his child who "grows more gorgeously like you." The comfort these two poems bring—and Gioia's impeccable work proclaims—is knowing that endings are hardly Endings. That mistakes can't only be seen as accidents: mistakes, too, are lives unanticipated—miracles.

———————————————

Linda Gregg

from *All of It Singing: New and Selected Poems*

TOO BRIGHT TO SEE

Just before dark the light gets dark. Violet
where my hands pull weeds around the Solomon's seals.
I see with difficulty what before was easy.
Perceive what I saw before
but with more tight effort. I am moon
to what I am doing and what I was.
It is a real beauty that I lived
and dreamed would be, now know
but never then. Can tell by looking hard,
feeling which is weed and what is form.
My hands are intermediary. Neither lover
nor liar. Sweet being, if you are anywhere that hears,
come quickly. I weep, face set, no tears, mouth open.

Tracy K. Smith on Linda Gregg's "Too Bright to See"

Very little in our human living is not about time. We parcel our hours and days, in this way meting out the matter of a lifetime. We conduct language so that it might gather up, circle back to, dodge, and circumscribe all the many things we are not satisfied to have experienced but once. For this reason, it often feels to me that poetry is a means of protest against—and also a momentary form of intervention upon—the pattern of fleeting experience and accumulating loss.

Linda Gregg's "Too Bright to See" bears witness to the metaphysical disorientation of living inside of time. For the poem's speaker, working in her garden at dusk, familiar temporal markers like minutes and hours are replaced with gradations of light, dark, and perceptible color. Descending through the poem's first five lines, we witness this diminishment of clarity intensify.

And then, the poem leaps. The terms of observation give way to a metaphor—"I am moon / to what I am doing and what I was." The speaker is wresting weeds from a garden plot while wrestling with the larger psychic task of self-integration. She is different in this instant from the person she only recently was. Yet she cannot see clearly back to that figure. She gets in her own way. This abstract task becomes ponderable by way of the weeds, the earth, the dwindling light, but its resolution remains elusive.

Why do I read "Too Bright to See" as a poem of consolation despite all the many forms of loss and diminishment that await? Because the speaker realizes that she can shift her address, and in so doing conjure a new understanding of her—our?—circumstance: "Sweet being, if you are anywhere that hears, / come quickly. I weep, face set, no tears, mouth open." She calls out across audible distance, as only the voice can do, and claims a grief that time—and light—have all but effaced.

John Haines

from *The Owl in the Mask of the Dreamer: Collected Poems*

WINTER NEWS

They say the wells
are freezing
at Northway where
the cold begins.

Old tins bang
as evening comes on
and clouds of
steaming breath drift
in the street.

Men go out to feed
the stiffening dogs,

the voice of the snowman
calls the white-
haired children home.

Dana Gioia on John Haines's "Winter News"

John Haines was an outsider, perhaps the ultimate literary outsider of his generation. He spent most of his life alone in the Alaskan wilderness. His homestead was so remote he claimed he could walk to the Arctic Ocean without seeing a road or human dwelling. The mystery is not that Haines survived the hardships of the arctic wastes. The wonder is that the decades of deprivation and isolation nurtured a profound and original writer.

The title poem of his debut collection, "Winter News," runs only fourteen short lines of free verse set in four irregular stanzas. It consists of forty-seven words, only one of them longer than two syllables. The words sit on a mostly white page. I doubt that Haines was trying to evoke the snowy northern landscape, but the arrangement puts his images in stark relief.

The images matter because the poem communicates mostly through its imagery—auditory and tactile as well as visual—without explanatory language. Northway, the only proper noun in the poem, is an actual place—an Alaskan settlement, with a population of about one hundred, mostly Native Americans, who call it Nabesna. A reader need not know any of that, however, to understand what a place named Northway means in the poem. It is a way into the cold. The landscape and the weather rule this world, and the humans—represented by a snowman and called "white-haired children"—have been transformed by the natural elements into new forms.

"Winter News" is not a big poem. I like that about it. It has a large resonance, but it remains local. The images feel permanent, primal, and real. The poem is a song to a cold country at the limits of human endurance. It offers neither praise nor criticism. It sings of things as they are.

Saskia Hamilton
  from *All Souls*

FARING

—

Light before you call it light graying the sky. Doves on window ledges call and answer, a low branching into seven-fold division.

'As' means *like* but also means *while*: As a cloud passes. As the shadow in the early morning. As the door turns on the hinge.

Who was it who said that every narrative is a soothing down.

Winter sun floods the table.

—

Quarter past ten: Wave of nausea after morning pills, hot tea, six candles. Thin sheets of cloud now dominant.

The boy wants glow sticks as protection.

Radiator—is it a hiss or a shush? An aspirant or a consolation? Half our days spent living in the future, an illusion.

Six days later: as the light grows, so does my will for the weight that tethers us to the ground, shoulder blades descending and meeting.

Flowers at once religious, secular, and sexual.

Blue sky, a dot of cloud. Voices of children from the street below; children with a ball.

Builders are raising the scaffolding, preparing their day's work. Talk with a friend, who was taken by the wolf at night.

—

Sediment on the windows, light flecks the edges of buildings, wind works at the building, worrying it, cyclist with a flickering lamp on the avenue below.

Shadow of a neighbor crosses the window in the building opposite.

—

Strength of feeling now vanished but the memory of it is of a kinship of some kind.

In its recollection, it registers unease beneath the day.

'I love you,' he says, 'but maybe we shouldn't profess our love for one another because, you know, it might mean you'll die?'

—

And what is actual? The word derives from a cauterizing agent, 'red-hot.' Is actual for one time only, as if only once could something be realized? In its weakened sense, it is 'opposed to potential, possible, ideal.' Beside me on the sofa, the boy is restless with joyous movement and intermittent improvised joy.

—

In the streets below, each passerby carries time internally, it opens the mind like a flower blown in its native bed.

William Cowper in his laundered kerchief at table. He stares out of the poem in alarm.

—

By rue d'Amsterdam, inside the rib of the building, crowds rush to three imminent trains, wait by the sandwich and coffee kiosk, trailed by wheeled luggage, pigeons, soldiers moving among them. The eye of the corporal passes over a bystanding neighbor.

Listings and times flap, click, shuffle, the building lists towards departure as if inclined to hear the far-off sound that marks the end of land.

Musical interlude, another train entering the great mouth.

Claudia Rankine on Saskia Hamilton's "Faring"

To read Saskia Hamilton's "Faring," the opening poem in her final collection *All Souls*, is to move through time in acts of seeing and noting what is seen. The morning ticks along as light enters to illuminate both the surrounding structure, window ledge, doves, as sounds seep in, wind, construction. To track the light, as the season moves into longer days, is to follow shadows of others moving here and there behind curtains across the way. The cyclical nature of dawn's return creates illusions of certainty for future days, though the speaker in "Faring" lives within an illness that names death its cure. This does not prevent love's negotiation with time, as a child withholds declarations of love in fear of time's retaliatory embrace. For now, the day seems to say, let the ordinary amaze, it's the grace we hold.

"Faring" builds its rooms against the "toomuchness" of life, life's actual, red-hot intensities, for fear that even the caring inquiry—How are you faring?—will no longer be a relevant question; or that the tracking of the gray morning sunrise will be the only relevant answer.

Like the eighteenth-century abolitionist poet William Cowper, who is called forward in "Faring" by his poem—the book open, perhaps, on the speaker's bedside table, like table talk—Hamilton rests her sights on what can be apprehended from a bed, sofa, chair, or window, and named in the quotidian. These small recognitions ensure a life's weightiness, wariness, worthiness. Three centuries after Cowper, it's not the countryside but the cityscape that allows Hamilton access to her own inner landscape.

The brilliance of "Faring," as well as its task, resides in its narrative charting of daily moments lived as "a soothing down."

THE CROWDS CHEERED AS GLOOM GALLOPED AWAY

Everyone was happier. But where did the sadness go? People wanted to know. They didn't want it collecting in their elbows or knees then popping up later. The girl who thought of the ponies made a lot of money. Now a month's supply of pills came in a hard blue case with a handle. You opened it & found the usual vial plus six tiny ponies of assorted shapes & sizes, softly breathing in the Styrofoam. Often they had to be pried out & would wobble a little when first put on the ground. In the beginning the children tried to play with them, but the sharp hooves nicked their fingers & the ponies refused to jump over pencil hurdles. The children stopped feeding them sugarwater & the ponies were left to break their legs on the gardens' gravel paths or drown in the gutters. On the first day of the month, rats gathered on doorsteps & spat out only the bitter manes. Many a pony's last sight was a bounding squirrel with its tail hovering over its head like a halo. Behind the movie theatre the hardier ponies gathered in packs amongst the cigarette butts, getting their hooves stuck in wads of gum. They lined the hills at funerals, huddled under folding chairs at weddings. It became a matter of pride if one of your ponies proved unusually sturdy. People would smile & say, "This would have been an awful month for me," pointing to the glossy palomino trotting energetically around their ankles. Eventually, the ponies were no longer needed. People had learned to imagine their sadness trotting away. & when they wanted something more tangible, they could always go to the racetrack & study the larger horses' faces. Gloom, #341, with those big black eyes, was almost sure to win.

Mary Jo Bang on Matthea Harvey's "The Crowds Cheered as Gloom Galloped Away"

Sometimes a poem achieves the near impossible, which is to make the reader marvel at how it works its magic while simultaneously having one's heart pierced by it. Or the top of one's head taken off, as Emily Dickinson described knowing something is poetry. Matthea Harvey's poem, via a digressive extended metaphor, takes the abstract and ineffable state of sorrow, a stable subject of lyric poetry (no pun intended), and concretizes it through a series of unlikely pairings of things. Tiny My Little Pony look-alikes live in the abyss of clinical depression; the Kentucky Derby occupies an upstairs room in the brick house where Dickinson was born; the world of teen movies hooks up with a theater alley with gum on the sidewalk. Oh, wait, those last two might actually belong together. In any event, *The Breakfast Club* meets *Prozac Nation* meets *The Belle of Amherst* meets Hasbro, Inc.'s toy franchise that features colorful ponies with names like Fluttershy and Pinkie Pie.

The poem plays not only with unlikely pairings but also with scale. Pill-sized anti-sadness ponies stand guard at the monumental ceremony for the cessation of life. This is that rare meeting where natural realism and the imagination sit down together and, after a bit of back and forth, agree that they really aren't all that different. Détente. It almost feels like a betrayal to talk about how the poem works. Literalizing the ineffable. Irony. Treating the exquisitely painful condition of abjection, which can range from feeling *meh* to contemplating suicide, with Beckettian humor. The brevity. As if Burton's nine-hundred-page *The Anatomy of Melancholy* had been reduced to a three-hundred-word thumbnail summary. And then the sly way poetry comes in at the end to insist that this apparently playful prose poem has an august lineage and the deepest of meanings: in Thomas H. Johnson's ordering of Dickinson's poems, the one that begins "After great pain, a formal feeling comes –" is #341, the same number as the long-faced horse that is said to be almost certain to win.

PRIMROSE FOR X

I was tracking Blake on Primrose Hill
one damp summer night.
Bundles of white chestnut flared
under the streetlights.

London's unsteady skyline
was not a reassuring one
but like a graph that measures
markets, snails and heartbeats.

When one brain was weary
one heart was not.
The brain can be shucked
when all the air is gone but the heart

is slippery and needs a touch of
spirit to nourish it.
How am I still here
at every thump?

The heart has its needs
and feelings sewn like threads
into branches and seasons
that we pencil as trees.

The Irish women with brass-capped hair
and tight mouths
and a Muslim woman with five girls and one boy
are all sadly clad at Victoria.

In poverty some screaming brats
are fat, and some are starved
into silence on their father's laps.
No father might be worse than that.

What is created by humans
is almost always alien.
The hissing buses and trains
in Kentish Town, boys hunched

in bunches on the lock
drugged and dirty and crushed
their eyes like lizards veiled
and blind in retreat while

a man with a machete
cut a fellow down, blood
all over his hands. Proud
of being a killing kind of man.

Machete or his father's hand: which one
caused this crime?
The aughts were grievous years
for boys and men.

Crowds of phantoms covered
Kent's fields as the Eurostar
raced away from London
and Blake's theophanies.

Jeffrey Yang on Fanny Howe's "Primrose for X"

William Blake once wrote to a friend that he conversed with the Spiritual Sun on Primrose Hill. Today his words saying as much are carved there on the stone curb atop a grassy knoll. Fanny Howe's "Primrose for X" opens with the poet "tracking Blake on Primrose Hill" and twelve quatrains later ends with her on a high-speed train that "raced away from London / and Blake's theophanies." What she finds in the lyric interim is the "unsteady skyline . . . / like a graph that measures / markets, snails and heartbeats"—one of many instances in Howe's poetry of her indwelling similization of the world around us. Meanings break free with snails and "shucked" at the end of the line that contrasts the brain with the "slippery" heart that also slips across the stanza. And how the vital heart monitor beats with the little line's cadence "How am I still here / at every thump?"—the question posed to herself or Thou of her own life's longevity answered by the steady pulse of spirit-touched heart, along with doubt's silence.

Here lines move in a spark with the restless "I," who finds the X subjects of love's gift among the poor immigrant women in Victoria, impoverished children, "drugged and dirty and crushed" boys of Kentish Town, and the victims of a father's violence, half-allegorized by a machete. Catherine Sophia Boucher Blake belongs here, too, in the hidden vision—she who learned the secrets and practice of her husband's illuminations and signed the parish register as bride with an "X."

The phantoms of the last stanza emerge out of the violent, "grievous years" as the poet speeds away in the darkness toward the unseen Channel. Phantoms or theophanies. These are the indecipherable forms of love Howe's words track and bring into impossible light—her poetry philophanies.

Ilya Kaminsky
from *Deaf Republic*

TO LIVE

To live is to love, the great book commands.
But love is not enough—

the heart needs a little foolishness!
For our child I fold the newspaper, make a hat

and pretend to Sonya that I am the greatest poet
and she pretends to be alive—

my Sonya, her stories and her eloquent legs,
her legs and stories that open other stories.

(*Stop talking while we are kissing!*)
I see myself—a yellow raincoat,

a sandwich, a piece of tomato between my teeth,
I hoist our infant Anushka to the sky—

(*Old fool*, my wife might have laughed)
I am singing as she pisses

on my forehead and my shoulders!

Catherine Barnett on Ilya Kaminsky's "To Live"

Varieties of ecstasy woven into Ilya Kaminsky's *Deaf Republic* deepen the lament, sharpen the protest. "To Live" opens with an aphorism from "the great book," followed by a correction: "But love is not enough— // the heart needs a little foolishness!" What follows seems, at first, playful: the speaker makes a hat for his daughter, then makes fun of his own pretensions—"[I] pretend to Sonya that I am the greatest poet." To this buoyant claim he adds, as if what follows is commensurate: "and she pretends to be alive—." That dash carries unspeakable loss. As does the seemingly lighthearted "pretend," which is—like other forms of *ecstasis*—a "standing outside the self."

One great pleasure of *Deaf Republic* is Kaminsky's metaphors, even when what they convey is tragic. In "To Live," we find Sonya's "eloquent legs," which, like her stories, "open other stories." The metaphor, chiasmus, and impossible present tense of this couplet bring death and erotic ecstasy into the same room. Later, the speaker describes himself—"a yellow raincoat, // a sandwich, a piece of tomato between my teeth"—a self-portrait drawn by someone who, propelled by grief, looks back at himself, dissociated: another form of ecstasy.

I find the last image of "To Live" so unexpected and moving: father and child left on their own in a scene of domestic hilarity. The verb "pisses" reaches back up sonically to "kissing" and "foolishness." Is this tender bumbling care for and celebration of what remains a baptism? Tears?

In later poems in *Deaf Republic*, the speaker gets carried away by soldiers, then publicly hanged. But in another kind of *ecstasis*— speaking from the afterlife—his voice remains, as an *ars poetica*: "*We must speak not only of great devastation.*" Kaminsky's ecstasy resides in the absent "but also," which in his work shows up everywhere.

Donika Kelly
from *The Renunciations*

The moon rose over the bay. I had a lot of feelings.

The home I've been making inside myself started
with a razing, a brush clearing, the thorn and nettle,
the blackberry bush falling under the bush hog.

Then I rested, a cycle fallow. Said *winter*. Said *the ground
is too cold to break, pony*. Said *I almost set fire
to it all, lit a match, watched it ghost in the wind*.

Came the thaw, came the melting snowpack, the flooded river,
new ground water, the well risen. I stood in the mud field
and called it a pasture. Stood with a needle in my mouth

and called it a song. Everything rushed past my small ears:
whir in the leaves, whir in the wing and the wood. *About time
to get a hammer*, I thought. *About time to get a nail and saw*.

Danez Smith on Donika Kelly's "The moon rose over the bay.
I had a lot of feelings."

In the final poem in her stellar, heroic, and zoetic collection *The
Renunciations*, Donika Kelly begins with what I imagine has been the
catalyst for many artists since humans first rose into language and
began putting symbols on cave walls. "The moon rose over the bay. I
had a lot of feelings." Honestly, that's camp. A wink inside of a famil-
iar and human scene: the poet stands in the presence of nature and
awe sends them inward.

What follows under that winking title is a poet making nature and
farmland out of her interiority, Kelly's speaker clearing the brush,
barely making it out of winter (who of us doesn't feel like igniting the
dark and frigid days of February?), and arriving at the softening of
spring and the possibility of summer. Four seasons captured in tercets,
in them a secret almanac for how to stay alive and rebuild after the
dark years.

The Renunciations practices a release fortified by bravery and ar-
tistic rigor and, like a gift at the end of what is hard-won in this col-
lection, here at last is this poem that reminds us that after all that
razing, the many deaths of our winters, and the violent seasons we
move through—regular and timely as the moon—still comes spring
with water and bloom and possibility.

Thank you, Donika, for reminding me that at the end of my sea-
sons waits my hammer. Thank you for pointing through the winter
toward the tools we can use to build us back.

———————————————

INPATIENT

The young attendants wrapped him in a red
velour blanket, and pulled the strapping taut.
Sedated on the stretcher and outside
for the last time, he raised his head and sniffed
the air like an animal. A wedge of geese
flew honking over us. The sky leaned close;
a drop of rain fell on his upturned face.
I stood aside, steward of Grandma's red-
letter New Testament and an empty vase.
The nurse went with him through the sliding door.
Without having to speak of it we left
the suitcase with his streetclothes in the car.

Tess Gallagher on Jane Kenyon's "Inpatient"

Much can be said about the strength of being that allowed Jane Kenyon to share her sadness and dismay that life required some heavy lifting. It was her bravery not to pretend, and she didn't. She let one feel the burden that simply living can be. The lighter side of Jane was mostly submerged in her poems, for she admired the steely gong of Anna Akhmatova's work, which she had translated.

Kenyon's poem "Inpatient" carries the patient and its readers inexorably away on a stretcher toward a destination from which we are given to understand he is unlikely to return. The phrase so telling of this is "he raised his head and sniffed / the air like an animal." The patient has been left to his keen animal awareness.

Next Kenyon adds sound and sight from the inpatient's point of view on his back: "A wedge of geese / flew honking over us." She has set it up for the tender "sky leaned close; / a drop of rain fell on his upturned face." We feel his utter helplessness and that drop of rain seems to fall right out of the poem onto our own faces.

Then, in the final line, the stunning collusion of a nurse and the speaker: "Without having to speak of it we left / the suitcase with his street clothes in the car."

Such a feeling of doom attends here, but also a silent reprieve for those having to perform these actions. They are in agreement about what is ahead of this patient, someone who won't be needing street clothes. It is a mark of the poem's strength that it continues to haunt by making its readers accessories to this unspoken omission. In so many poems, what one is silent about drives the emotional power.

Vénus Khoury-Ghata
translated from the French by Marilyn Hacker
from *She Says*

In those days   I know now   words declaimed the wind
besides pebbles there were moons but no lamps
the stars would emerge later from a brawl between two flintstones

I'll tell you everything there were five pebbles
one for each continent
vast enough   to contain a child of a different color

So there were   five children but no houses
windows but no walls
wind but no streets
the first man wore a stone around his neck

He made an arrangement with the first tree
an oak if I remember correctly
the one who got there first could drink up the ocean

Language at that time was a straight line reserved for birds
the letter "i" was the cleft of a female hummingbird
"h" a ladder with one rung necessary to replace a charred sun before
    nightfall
"o" a hole in the sole of the universe

Unlike the consonants with their rough garments
the vowels were naked
all the weaver's art consisted of humoring them
in the evening they counted each other to make sure no one was
    missing
in the rocky countries men slept without dreaming

Ilya Kaminsky on Vénus Khoury-Ghata's "In those days
I know now   words declaimed the wind," translated from
the French by Marilyn Hacker

Vénus Khoury-Ghata was born in Lebanon in 1937 and immigrated
to Paris in 1972. When asked why she writes in French, she responded,
"to reinvent Lebanon as it was before the war, before death." In a time
of death and destruction in my birth country, Ukraine, I come back
to Khoury-Ghata's sequence "Words," from which this poem is a part.

I am intrigued by how, on one side, there is a logical narrative
structure at the start of each stanza: "In those days," "I'll tell you every-
thing," "So there were," "Language at that time was." On the other
side, there is a magical landscape delivered via figurative language:
"words declaimed the wind," "the stars would emerge later from a brawl
between two flintstones," "there were five pebbles / one for each con-
tinent." This tension between the structures of narrative and imag-
ery appeals to me. Then, there is the tension of negation: "there were
moons, but no lamps," "five children but no houses / windows but no
walls / wind but no streets." Finally, there is a tension between specif-
ics of numbers ("two flintstones," "five pebbles," "one for each," "five
children," "first man," "first tree") and specifics of letters ("i," "h," "o"),
as well as specifics of image-rich nouns: "flintstones," "humming-
bird," "ladder," "garments." These tensions keep readers on their toes,
and provide this poem with its dreamlike, mythic atmosphere.

In the aftermath of war, Khoury-Ghata wants to begin anew, but
metaphors that build her new world do not feel like literary embel-
lishments; they insist on something *primal*: one senses one is reading
Arabic folklore clashed with French surrealism, yes, but the last word
is never Breton's. Making new myths in the aftermath of war, her figu-
rative language feels like a beautiful construction that might other-
wise need to be expressed by a scream.

Larry Levis
from *The Darkening Trapeze*

NEW YEAR'S EVE AT THE SANTA FE HOTEL, FRESNO, CALIFORNIA

for Bruce & Marsha

Smoke, laughter, & a bar whose solemn oak
Has outlasted worse times than my own . . .
In the ballroom of their last hotel, whole families
Of Basques had come again to dance, slowly,
Some austere polka nobody but Basques
Had ever seen, or learned. Once a year
I come back to this place, embrace friends,
And drink to what got lost in bad translation:
The town we tried to change, changed anyway.
The street we blocked off on a warm day
In 1970 is lined with cute
Boutiques, & that girl, once queen
Of her high-school prom, who two years later
Left to harvest sugarcane in Cuba,
Works late tonight, taking inventory:
So many belts, so many sandals sold.
Then jogging five miles home before she sleeps.

We drank Fundador late, & I went out
Alone in the cold New Year to find
No one on the street, no trains
Pausing in their own breath in the depot
Behind the hotel, no soldier, & no lovers
Either. What I heard & saw were a hundred
Sparrows gathering in one small tree,
Their throats full of some ridiculous

Joy or misery at being sparrows, winged,
Striped, & handicapped for life. I thought
That coming back here always showed me just
How much this place has changed; but no. The only
Real change is me. Now, when I sit
Across from two friends at a table, I am
Whatever's distant, snow beginning to fall
On the plains; a thief's fire. Someday I won't
Be home to anyone. Some days, it takes
Two hours of careful talk before I'm me
Again. I miss that talk, although I think
I'm right to be alone, in the gift of my
One life, listening to songs not made
For me, invented by no one I know, for luck,
For a winter night, for two friends who,
Some nights, some days, gave me everything.

Mai Der Vang on Larry Levis's "New Year's Eve at the Santa Fe Hotel, Fresno, California"

Trains. Sparrows. Nights. Fresno. I'm drawn into the way Larry Levis imbues the setting and physical milieu with bittersweet loneliness, especially in a poem about friendship. As a Fresno native, I know this area in downtown of which he writes. I have heard its breath in the day, a bustling city center where people walk and drive with purpose, somewhere to go, someone to meet. But I have also seen these streets empty of government workers and pedestrians by nightfall. Transformation into a ghost town. Brick factories. Abandoned warehouses. Unlit offices.

Today, the Santa Fe Hotel has been gentrified into an upscale, boutique inn, and the Basque restaurant has relocated to another area of town. But the train depot remains, and it is a place I know well. Throughout my undergraduate years, I caught the Amtrak there from Fresno to Berkeley in what became an ever-constant life pattern of zigzagging travel. As Levis depicts, "no trains / Pausing in their own breath in the depot / Behind the hotel," these places of transit seem to be haunted by an absence, a nothingness that stays behind and can no longer be grasped after the leaving has happened. I'm reminded of the many times I departed Fresno by train, saying farewell to family, then looking forward, fighting the urge to turn and glance back.

Levis was born in Fresno, and he's right: "I thought / That coming back here always showed me just / How much this place has changed; but no. The only / Real change is me." Maybe it's never about the place but about the absence of the self in that place. That this is among his last poems adds even more ache to the absence: "Someday I won't / Be home to anyone. . . . / I think / I'm right to be alone, in the gift of my / One life." Stunning. In such Levis spirit. And what a gift of a life it was.

Liu Xiaobo
translated from the Chinese by Jeffrey Yang
from *June Fourth Elegies*

FOR SU BINGXIAN

> *At home in Beijing, 1/17/2001*
> *Eleventh anniversary offering for 6/4*

1

The sudden news of your passing
arrived in winter with a rare heavy snowfall
that draped the foulness of Beijing
in a temporary disguise
At Tiananmen Square an armed policeman on
watch used his leather boot to kick and break
apart a child's snowman piled up high

11 years ago
your child your son
was just like that snowman
smashed by the pure wretchedness of bullets
After the echoes of gunfire
fear spread through everyone's minds
Surveillance devices also recorded
the wails and the weeping

2

Forbidden to grieve
Forbidden to recollect

Forbidden for the mother who lost her son
to visit the wife who lost her husband
Forbidden for the young paraplegic
sitting in a wheelchair, to receive
an arm of support for him to walk
Forbidden for the widow
to receive a bouquet of flowers
Forbidden for the orphan
to be given a new book-bag
Forbidden for warm hands to help
the wronged ghost with no home to return to
with just a handful of dirt to plant a green patch
Strictly forbidden for the few forlorn eyes left
to seek the executioners in their lawful hiding places
Forbidden forbidden forbidden forbidden . . .
11 years ago
it was forbidden for a drop of rain
to fall on this cracked tortoise-shell earth
11 years later
it is forbidden for the snowman the child piled
up to live out its brief life

3

Snowfall
generation after generation
of wronged ghosts pile up
The ice-clear jade pureness
is an illusory semblance
When the sun comes out
heaps of trash
flood memory full

A bayonet
can cleave body from shadow
sever snowflake from earth
yet cannot split apart the candle flames from the night
Any form of memorial
for what was once impassioned blood
is inevitably too pale
The wrinkles of the Mothers
turn spilt blood into snow-thick skies
for the figures of the graves to soar into

4

Concerning death
whatever I say
can be no more than
your eyes just before dying
each stirring-still glance
will be no less than the first
last day of judgment

Su Bingxian: Mother of twenty-one-year-old Zhao Long, a demonstrator during the June Fourth Movement who was found shot three times in the chest.

Harryette Mullen on Liu Xiaobo's "For Su Bingxian," translated from the Chinese by Jeffrey Yang

Writing against, around, and through official silence, Liu Xiaobo (1955–2017) memorialized the events in Tiananmen Square on June 4, 1989, a political protest the state violently crushed and rigorously erased from its official history. Refusing to forget, declining to be silent about the demonstrators' fates, Liu built a monument of defiant memory, writing poems for every anniversary of the protest. Collected and translated with commentary by Jeffrey Yang, *June Fourth Elegies* brought Liu's poetry to the attention of readers in the United States.

When Liu was awarded the Nobel Peace Prize in 2010, he was serving his fourth prison term in China. As his country's most prominent dissident and most famous political prisoner, Liu was not allowed to attend the award ceremony. The state embargoed news of his prize, prompting creative expression among Liu's admirers. In his absence, the gold peace medal was placed on the empty seat reserved for Liu at the Nobel ceremony in Oslo. Forbidden to mention his name, ingenious social media users in China resorted to metonymy, circulating images of an unoccupied chair, or characters for "empty chair," referring to Liu's distinguished honor while evading official censors. Responding to Liu's Nobel win with the comment "   " a fellow Chinese writer activated the blank space between quotation marks to signify more than silence. Years later, we read reports of police seizing from the people's hands blank placards they held up to protest state censorship. Following this creative form of dissent, the artist Ai Weiwei began to autograph blank paper with invisible ink.

The snowman destroyed in Liu's 2001 poem remains as the nothing that is. In the spirit of Liu Xiaobo, imaginative protesters in China and elsewhere express dissent, understanding that silence is an obstacle, but not a deterrent.

VAPORATIVE

However a light may come
through vaporative
glass pane or dry dermis
of hand winter bent
I follow that light
capacity that I have
cup-sized capture
snap-like seizure I
remember small
is less to forget
less to carry
tiny gears mini-
armature I gun
the spark light
I blink eye blink
at me to look
at me in
light eye
look twice
and I eye
alight
again.

—

When I want to write seriously I think of people like
dg for whom I wrote a long poem for whom I revised
until the poem forgot its way back troubled I let it go when
you love something let it go if it returns be a good mother
father welcome the poem open armed pull out the frying
pan grease it coat it prepare a meal
apron and kitchen sweat labor
my love my sleeves pushed
to elbows like the old days a sack
of flour and keys I push them
typography and hotcakes work
seduce a poem into believing
I can home it I can provide it
white gravy whatever the craving
poem eat and lie down full
poem rest here full don't
lift a single l
etter.

—

Strange how lying on this side works
yet on my back I grieve and turning
to my left I rewind to a child's world
so I re-turn back over to the first
position of poesis prenascent page
before any material thing makes
in this right-side peace I work most
nights I greet open-eyed delicate
pronunciations like *thank you* I thank
the empty room I still my body I work hard
not to slip a centimeter in dark work not to
interrupt my own conversation I move
my mouth as if silently reading as if a begin
ner or courting a friendship careful holding
to my chest small gifts tight 3-lettered
words in 3-word phrases I welcome in
the new new.

—

promise:

if I read you
what I wrote bear
in mind I wrote it

down only
so   *that*
I remember

—

example:

I have always wanted *opaque* to mean see-through, transparent. I'm
    disheartened to learn

it means the opposite. Why this instinct to assign a definition based
    on sound. *O-PĀK—*

I interpret O: open / P: soft / Ā: airplane or directional flight / K:
    cut through—translating to

that which is or allows air, airy, penetrating light, transparency.
    To say, you don't fool me

for a second you're opaque. To say, I'm partial to opaque objects I
    delight in luminosity. To say,

I'm interested in this painting on glass brightly opaque. I understand
    the need to define

as a need for stability. That I and you can be things, standing
    understood, among each other.

One word can be a poem believe it, one word can destroy a poem
    dare I. Say I am writing

to penetrate the opaque but I confuse it too often. I negotiate instinct
    when a word of lightful

meaning flips under / buries me in the work of blankets.

—

A poem about writing, *bo-ring.* Says my contemporary artistic companionate, a muscular observation and I agree. A poem about writing poems, how. Boring as it is, it asks me to do. I couldn't any other thing tonight. I sat I wrote about writing. I write I sit about writing. I'm about to write about it, writing and sitting. I will write and sit with my writing.

Defamiliarize your writing then, somebody says okay I'm not sitting then I say to somebody. I'm chewing at a funeral and. I'm nibbling my pulp knuckles. I'm watching a man with a stain on his. Pants always wrinkle in this heat, gnats and humidity. I walk to the front pew to make a lewd, joke. I regard laughter from the man in the. Pants are always honest I mean really heavy at a summer burial. Yet he doesn't ever cry, the stained man, why. When I observe nothing (unusual) I do nothing (unusual) in response. New or novel. Real lit relics on these occasions. In ritual: nobody's learning, true. And to lewd is dumb, likewise. Like the way I put up my dukes when I observe the cowboy kneel. He's praying he's asking. He doesn't see me, my gesture's futile. What am I doing here, writing. What am I doing here righting the page at funerals.

—

When I stay up late I have thoughts, continually pen-marked by the
    clicking-on

of an air-conditioner a cutting coolness the imbalance I hear so clearly

in critique. Yet nuance saves a line and looking / space / in the trees,
    I watch our dog

bounce carrying the bone of a sheep's leg. I notice the carcass and her
    bark: both absent.

So I learn to write around it, the meat, in wide circles to be heard.
    When a friend says

I believe you're privileged by being so closely under, I ruffle I ease.
    It's not easy.

Who'm I speaking to so often no one if not the friend. On the road to
    Shiprock I count

eight dust devils spiraling at once in proximity all in, a line. Then
    only seven.

What causes reduction in this instance? I'm tempted by the bed next
    to my desk, yet

the desk next to my bed "sounds" better sometimes. I don't want to
    hear a fiction writer say,

This is why I don't read poetry. I mean, he said it not me. Of course:
    influence(s). Where do I

consider myself among them she asks. A tick head burrows in the
skin of a question. I glue

a coffee cup to my lips, blow the heat. The sun's not up yet the birds
begin first

5:06 a.m. A signal. Lie down closely my skin to sheet and pillow now
the eyes orbit

the white star of a Caps Lock light STOP don't revise a word comma
semicolon or.

Erin Marie Lynch on Layli Long Soldier's "Vaporative"

Short lines assembled into a narrow shard. Facing stanzas, ragged like torn paper. Three brief phrases, held apart. A breathless, long-limbed passage, spilling into the margins. Reading "Vaporative," I move through seven shapes of thought, seven configurations of an ars poetica. Here, in so many ways, Layli Long Soldier asks the poem: *What are you? Who are you for? What can you do?* This is a poem about poems about writing, each surprising formal turn chipping away at the claim that such concerns are "*bo-ring.*"

"Vaporative" constructs a crowded inner landscape, noisy with voices. The speaker's friends appear as collaborators and interlocutors. A fiction writer sneers at poetry; a man in stained pants laughs at a funeral. The poem itself transforms into a runaway child, a small gift, a luminous and opaque object. And then the "you," reaching out to the reader: "if I read you / what I wrote bear / in mind I wrote it." These figures all trouble or inspire the speaker, prompting her to defamiliarize and define, to ruminate, reposition, and resist. A poem about writing, it turns out, is about everyone. "Vaporative" hints at the liberatory possibility pulsing through *WHEREAS*: poetic language, humming with collective life, can drown out the soulless drone of authoritarian speech.

On the last page, a small "spark light" from the poem's first movement comes back as "the white star of a Caps Lock light." The speaker grounds herself in the physical act of writing, her finger pressing the Caps Lock button as she types her final line: "STOP don't revise a word comma semicolon or." A poem about writing becomes, at last, a poem about not writing. That "or" leaves a final clause imagined— vaporative. Closing with a conjunction, the poem asks us to ask, *Or what?* Long Soldier offers us that *or*, a doorway opening into the un-written, and we step through.

Sally Wen Mao
from *Oculus*

ANNA MAY WONG GOES VIRAL

In the future, there's an oracle
        where you can search
for where you belong. I ask this engine
        and it replies:
do the deleted scenes choke you
        up? In the future, I am young
and poor, so I become a webcam girl.

On camera I read passages
        from Russian novels.
Curious netizens subscribe to my site
        then cancel, ranting on forums
about my prudish act, how no one wants
        to see a girl bend over
a thick book and wheeze.

After I go viral, I shut down my website.
        Screenshots circulate cyberspace—
Anna, dressed as a purple panda,
        Anna, taking a swig from a demitasse.

I collect all the passwords to my shrines.
        I hack into them, grow a habit
of Photoshopping hyena spots onto
        my own skin and uploading
my spoiled face onto Instagram.

My complexion has the mottle
　　　　of century eggs. My mustaches grow
feather tufts. I replace the paillettes
　　　　on my gowns with scales.
Recently, on the red carpet, I wear dresses
　　　　made of kelp, breathe
through fake gills and carry plastic
　　　　sacs full of saltwater.

Soon a crop of young girls will join me,
　　　　renouncing their dresses to wade
in the thrill of being animal.

Matthea Harvey on Sally Wen Mao's "Anna May Wong Goes Viral"

By the time you read "Anna May Wong Goes Viral" in Sally Wen Mao's *Oculus,* you've already encountered the first Chinese American 1920s movie star in ten previous poems in a myriad of imagined scenarios. "Anna May Wong Goes Viral" is her last appearance in the book, and it features a final star-turn transformation. Sometime in the not-so-distant future, Wong performs a kind of send-up of the work of webcam girls, choosing only to share live video of herself reading novels. Razor-sharp line breaks showcase Mao's sly wit: "do the deleted scenes choke you / up?" and "no one wants / to see a girl bend over / a thick book and wheeze."

After Wong goes viral on the internet, she turns away from the digital commodification of beauty by enacting another type of artificial virality—she defaces images of herself on Instagram by "Photoshopping hyena spots onto / my own skin." Mao's imagination doesn't stop there—instead Wong makes her fashion interventions a reality, appearing on the red carpet in a kelp dress and fake gills (it's hard not to picture some recent Met Gala looks). At this point, she envisions herself as a kind of Pied Piper for young girls, who will cast off their clothes and join her to embrace "the thrill of being animal."

I taught this poem (published in 2019) remotely in 2020, when the world went viral in the original sense. My students and I were missing the comfort of being animals in a room together. Our lives were more online than ever, and when we were out in the world, the masks we were wearing felt a bit like Wong on the runway, breathing through "fake gills."

from *Trimmings* by Harryette Mullen

from *Recyclopedia*

Mistress in undress, filmy peignoir. Feme sole in camisole. Bit part, petite cliché. Dégagé ladies lingering, careless of appurtenances. Longing pajamas, custom worn to disrobe. Froufrou negligee, rustling silk, or cattle. Negligent in ladies' lingerie, a dressy dressing down.

Monica Youn on Harryette Mullen's *Trimmings*

Harryette Mullen is always the first poet on my syllabus when I'm teaching poetic craft. Few poets make us understand so viscerally and so multidimensionally what it means for us—as artists—to be working with the English language as a primary artistic medium. That we are speaking and writing in English at all—and within an English language poetic tradition—is a fact that we cannot afford to take for granted. We know from Audre Lorde that "the master's tools will never dismantle the master's house," but how can we come to terms with the realization that the English language, historically speaking, is the master's tools? But in Mullen's hands, these tools undermine, excavate, perforate, dislodge, renovate—hollowing out breathing space, elbow room, fashioning a home within an often inhospitable tradition.

In her essay "African Signs and Spirit Writing," Mullen traces a heritage of visionary textuality among the artistic techniques of enslaved African Americans, who were often practically and legally barred from pursuing conventional literacy—"writing 'in the spaces' of the master's copybook," collagist syncretisms, ritual spirit writing and glossolalia. We see traces of this heritage in this marvelously multilayered little snippet from *Trimmings*, Mullen's effort to come to terms with Gertrude Stein's literary legacy in a volume originally published on Lee Ann Brown's Tender Buttons Press. In her preface to *Recyclopedia*, the Graywolf reissue of three of her early collections, Mullen writes that she "found an entry" into Stein's work through her story "Melanctha," a work that implanted the stereotype of the "tragic mulatto" firmly in the modernist tradition and whose often obsessive racism makes it hard to get through. Mullen takes this unpromising material and fashions a kind of performance in pentimenti, in which clichés of decadence, dominance, and animalistic sensuality create their own shadow play of echo and suggestion, a slyly seductive dance of resistance and reclamation.

Alice Oswald

from *Spacecraft Voyager 1: New and Selected Poems*

SEA SONNET

A field, a sea-flower, three stones, a stile.
Not one thing close to another
throughout the air. The cliff's uplifted lawns.
You and I walk light as wicker in virtual contact.

Prepositions lie exposed. All along
the swimmer is deeper than the water.
I have looked under the wave,
I saw your body floating on the darkness.

Oh time and water cannot touch.
Not touch. Only a blob far out,
your singularity and the sea's
inalienable currents flow at angles ...

and if I love you this is incidental
as on the sand one blue towel, one white towel.

Mary Szybist on Alice Oswald's "Sea Sonnet"

When my understanding of someone close to me begins to slow to an uncomfortable stillness, I may find myself reaching for a poem by Alice Oswald. Sometimes I reach for her quiet and restless "Sea Sonnet," a love poem and an almost love poem, an experience of language almost as dizzyingly unsteady and alive as, it reminds me, real relating.

The poem begins in stillness. Opening with a fragment, a list of nouns allows each one to float next to but separate from the others, their relationships undirected by prepositions or verbs. Stiles are usually in fields, but here "field" and "stile" float at opposite ends of the line, "a sea-flower" and "three stones" between them. One hardly notices the familiar ways prepositions govern relations until one experiences their absence. To linger in a line without them is to then be better prepared to hear the relationships proposed by *throughout* and *along* and *under*. "Prepositions lie exposed," each one seeming to clarify the relationship between things— and yet, they "lie." It's less that they deliberately deceive than that they can't keep up, can't quite make contact with or describe the shifting proximities between the speaker and the beloved.

It's in the wobbliness of the experience of closeness that the poem floats. It's a sonnet and also an anti-sonnet. There's no thought that carries the speaker closer to the beloved, no achieved transformation. A strengthened connection is not worked toward, or discovered, or revealed. Love happens, if it happens, *to* or *in* or *at* or *on* or, like the two towels, *beside*. It happens in happenstance, within the "inalienable currents" in which we drift.

"Sea Sonnet" inhabits those currents while a feeling of intimacy glints through its lines: though "your body [is] floating on the darkness" and I see you from "under a wave," I recognize that "the swimmer is deeper than the water." This poem leaves me feeling ready to be present to who and what may not be as close as they seem, present to what I cannot orchestrate, to the luck and possibility of incident.

THE RAT

A young man wrote a poem about a rat.
It was the best poem ever written about a rat.
To read it was to ask the rat to perch
on the arm of your chair until you turned the page.
So we wrote to him, but heard nothing; we called,
and called again; then finally we sailed
to the island where he kept the only shop
and rapped his door until he opened up.

We took away his poems. Our hands shook
with excitement. We read them on lightboxes,
under great lamps. They were not much good.
So then we offered what advice we could
on his tropes and turns, his metrical comportment,
on the wedding of the word to the event,
and suggested that he might read this or that.
We said *Now: write us more poems like The Rat.*

All we got was cheek from him. Then silence.
We gave up on him. Him with his green arrogance
and ingratitude and his one lucky strike.
But today I read The Rat again. Its reek
announced it; then I saw its pisshole stare;
line by line it strained into the air.
Then it hissed. *For all the craft and clever-clever*
you did not write me, fool. Nor will you ever.

Tom Sleigh on Don Paterson's "The Rat"

Contradiction, progression through contraries, a faith that quickness, irony, and wit can carry you farther than high-minded drumrolls, soapbox earnestness, all too self-conscious "witnessing"—these are qualities that Don Paterson, the much-lauded Scottish poet, has cultivated throughout his writing life. His own comment on the poem, "I suppose I think of 'The Rat' as a not very good poem about a very good poem," exemplifies Paterson's slyness, humor, and self-skepticism. Is it a political poem in rat's clothing? A comment on what Seamus Heaney once called the "Absolute Speaker" at the center handing down, ex cathedra, acceptable aesthetics, manners, and morals to the Young Poet writing in isolation on his peripheral little island?

But the satire cuts both ways: by the end of the poem, when the rat unexpectedly shows up and has its own say, it tells off both the Absolute Speaker and the Young Poet—the latter for hubris in imagining he can capture "ratness"; the former for assuming it has the right to judge what "ratness" is.

The idiom of "The Rat" is an anomaly in Paterson's work overall: stripped down, pushing against rhetorical flourish, the slant rhymed couplets falling unemphatically, the meter roughened up, yet subtly underpinning the concatenating ironies. Much has been made, rightly, of Paterson's virtuosity—but it's his perennial disenchantment with his own rhetorical spells that makes him such a galvanizing, unpredictable, pleasurable poet. For Paterson, the sine qua non of poetry is to be radically unstable, a way of rebelling against "*the craft and clever-clever.*" Of course, if you can't do "*the craft and clever-clever,*" you don't have much of anything. But the rat's "reek" and "pisshole stare" takes a rat's-eye view of things—local, provisional, always on the hunt.

Carl Phillips
from *Pastoral*

PARABLE

There was a saint once,
he had but to ring across
water a small bell, all

manner of fish
rose, as answer, he was
that holy, persuasive,

both, or the fish
perhaps merely
hungry, their bodies

a-shimmer with
that hope especially that
hunger brings, whatever

the reason, the fish
coming unassigned, in
schools coming

into the saint's hand and,
instead of getting,
becoming food.

I have thought, since, of
your body—as I first came
to know it, how it still

can be, with mine,
sometimes. I think on
that immediate and last gesture

of the fish leaving water
for flesh, for guarantee
they will die, and I cannot

rest on what to call it.
Not generosity, or
a blindness, trust, brute

stupidity. Not the soul
distracted from its natural
prayer, which is attention,

for in the story they are
paying attention. They
lose themselves eyes open.

Fanny Howe on Carl Phillips's "Parable"

In his poem "Parable," Carl Phillips glides into his subject from many angles. He begins with a saint and follows with a bell—his summons to fish to come and be eaten. No bait, hook, or sinker for this saint who uses his hand to capture what is really almost only a glimmer of light. I think this must be the poet's only vision when he began the poem, since Phillips is a wandering thinker: his thoughts can go far suddenly.

Jesus was a fisher of men and could also provide fish and bread to multitudes of people who needed food. A parable begins with real persons and their needs and errors. This poem is composed of subtle hunger and human needs, and reminds me of the thinking of Simone Weil when she talks about necessity and about attention. She wrote: "Attention, taken to its highest degree, is the same thing as prayer. It presupposes faith and love."

To catch a fish, full attention must be given to the dark water and small clues as to where a school or one individual fish will go. The poem suddenly jumps and becomes a parable about love, desire, and touch. For Phillips, the fish conjures up a memory of a person he touched and loved. His full attention goes to this encounter, then shifts back to the saint and the fish.

What he has noticed is "Not the soul / distracted from its natural / prayer, which is attention," but the spontaneous movement of the fish, eyes wide open, into the hand of the saint. There it will become food. It will be obedient and will not resist being caught. The poet and the poem have done the same. This must be love.

BOONIES

Where we could be boys together. This region of want:
the campestrial flat. The adolescents roving across the plat.
        Come hither. He-of-the-hard would call me hither.

Sheer abdomen, sheer slickensides, the feldspar buttes
·that mammillate the valley right where it needs to bust.

And I could kiss his tits and he could destroy me
        on the inflorescent slopes; in his darkest dingles;
upon the grassland's raffish plaits. And he could roll me
        in coyote brush: I who was banished to the barren
                could come back into his fold, and I
        would let him lay me down on the cold, cold ground.

Clouds, above, lenticular, the spreading fundament,
        a glorious breech among the thunderheads
and in their midst, a great white heron magnifies
                the day. We'd keep together, he and I,
and we'd gain meaning from our boyage; we'd pursue
        each other through the crush of darkling rifts.
                Climb into each other's precipitous coombes.

Where would it end, this brush and bush, this brome
        and blazing star? There is always some new way
                to flex a limb and find its secret drupe.

        Not only the hope of nature; the nature of hope:

so long as culverts carry us, so long as we stay ripe
        to one another's lips, and welcoming to hands,
as long as we extend our spans, to tangle them,
              as spinning insects do their glistered floss.

This is not a time to think the trumpet vine is sullen.
Rather: the trumpet's bell is but a prelude.
        It says we all are beautiful at least once.
And, if you'd watch over me, we can be beautiful again.

Diane Seuss on D. A. Powell's "Boonies"

"Boonies" contains everything I want from a poem. It's an epic accordioned into thirty lines. An epic of what? Unmonitored spaces. Boonies, where we exist outside the town's jurisdiction. "Where we could be boys together." Queer spaces expressed in geology/geography. Want is a region. Desire is somewhere.

What teases and teaches me in this poem is D. A. Powell's masterful control of an accretion of diction types, each derived from a different source. It offers a wellspring of geological language: slickenside, butte, mammillate, dingle, fundament, coombe, brome, and drupe, to name but a few. The language is accurate to its source while doing erotic double duty, performing sonic sexiness and double entendre. "Sheer abdomen, sheer slickensides, the feldspar buttes / that mammillate the valley right where it needs to bust." The fourteen-year-old in me snickers. The landscape junkie swoons.

Each stanza extends the "boyage," a voyage into meaning, and the music thereof. I hear Keats ("Where would it end, this brush and bush, this brome / and blazing star?"), the euphoniousness of Dylan Thomas ("his darkest dingles; / upon the grassland's raffish plaits"), and something of the lost World War I soldier ("I / would let him lay me down on the cold, cold ground"). A single-line stanza rings loudly: "Not only the hope of nature; the nature of hope." And with that moment, I feel the mournful hopefulness of disappearing landscapes. Not nostalgia, but a homesickness for my own boonies and the trouble I brewed.

God, we were beautiful. "And, if you'd watch over me, we can be beautiful again." This is sweet, fragrant, romantic, and rhetorical. Compassion, my darling. In all the years I've taught "Boonies," which is many, at least one blossoming late adolescent has had those words emblazoned on their body via an injudicious tattoo.

Claudia Rankine

from *Don't Let Me Be Lonely: An American Lyric*

Define loneliness?

Yes.

It's what we can't do for each other.

What do we mean to each other?

What does a life mean?

Why are we here if not for each other?

Solmaz Sharif on Claudia Rankine's *Don't Let Me Be Lonely*

When it happened, flags appeared everywhere, even in Berkeley's brown-shingle liberal respite. *Not in our name.* A kind of NIMBY-ism of national myth took over—*this* is America, it said: Tolerant. Peaceful. Wanting only justice. Wanting a controlled bloodletting. It was the America of President Obama a few years later, announcing in a rare use of active construction and absence of euphemism that the United States has "killed Osama bin Laden." On 9/12, one became aware of how many surfaces there are to announce "nation": car windows, storefronts, plastic bags, french fries. An estrangement of matter, of material.

Enter *Don't Let Me Be Lonely* and its many announcements: the thinness and length of the book sitting farther behind and taller than the others on the shelf. The long strip of white space left below its prose blocks. The photographs and the snow-filled TVs with Dubya's face vaguely in there. *An American Lyric.* Not Whitman's voracious parallel line, biblical in want and catalog, but the accumulative, declarative drone of doctor's notes, steno books, medicated grief—the clear-eyed recounting of what simply is, the lonelinesses at the end of the rail lines of earlier, selective possibility.

The slip of the answer, "Yes," to the arresting question, "Define loneliness?" The simple misattunements compounded, or else the medias res of the conversation we are all in and did not start. Our historical lives stripped back to two people speaking across a lunch table, a bulletproof cab window. The faces of James Byrd and Amadou Diallo. This book is one of the most powerful historical registers of the time, yes, and even more so, a masterwork in tone, in form, in a holistic temperature-taking of what it meant to be alive then, what it means to be alive at all. How many times have I asked myself why I am saying what I am saying, why I am doing what I am doing, and arrived at this book's title, its precise plea staring back at me?

Rainer Maria Rilke
translated from the French by A. Poulin, Jr.
from *The Complete French Poems of Rainer Maria Rilke*

CEMETERY

Is there an aftertaste of life in these graves? And in the flowers' mouths
do bees find the hint of a word refusing speech? O flowers, prisoners
of our instincts to be happy, do you come back to us with our dead in
your veins? Flowers, how can you escape our grip? How can you not
be *our* flowers? Does the rose use all its petals to fly away from us?
Does it want to be only a rose, nothing but rose? No one's sleep under
so many eyelids?

Mark Wunderlich on Rainer Maria Rilke's "Cemetery,"
translated from the French by A. Poulin, Jr.

Rainer Maria Rilke's French poems were assembled and translated
into English by A. Poulin, Jr., for the first time, and published by
Graywolf in 1986. The results are a revelation. Rilke, who is one of the
great lyric poets of the German language, produced a second body
of work in French of remarkable breadth and nuance. It should be no
surprise that many of these French poems take up the subjects, im-
ages, and symbols readers of the *Sonnets to Orpheus* and the *Duino
Elegies* would recognize: angels, animals, the secret lives of objects, and
of course, the dead who, Rilke reminds us, do not need us at all.

In his prose poem "Cemetery," Rilke opens with two questions as
he contemplates the flowers that grow among the graves of a church-
yard. He asks us to imagine the rosebush sending its roots deep into the
earth, bringing out some essence of those people buried deep under-
ground, around whom the roots might tangle. He moves on to sympa-
thize with the rose—symbolic object of so much human fascination
and attention—and wonders if the rose doesn't want to be just itself,
liberated from our desires and projections and uses. These reversals of
perspective are what make Rilke's late work so expansive, offering us
new ways to see the eternal and universal truths of human experience.

When Rilke was a young man, he wrote in his diary, "I invented
a new form of caress: placing a rose gently on a closed eye until its cool-
ness can no longer be felt; only the gentle petal will continue to rest on
the eyelid like sleep just before dawn." Years later, he was still cling-
ing to this image, still turning it over, imagining those roses as eyelids,
here closed forever in the sleep of the dead.

The epitaph on Rilke's grave also invokes the petals of roses being
like the lids of eyes, and so this prose poem selected here reads al-
most posthumously—as if Rilke—now in his grave—spoke to the
living and asked the very question of whether something of him was
being carried from the underworld up to the land of the living, blessed
as it is with sun, and flowers and bees.

BLUE

came late to
language once
we were

thrashing the sea
was wine-
dark flash

of wing
and nothing
was the same

the sea
kissed the
sky and now

day is then
night is
more what did

you lose
in becoming
family what

dazzling otherwise
do I name
when I

address you

Kaveh Akbar on Claire Schwartz's "Blue"

Reading Claire Schwartz, it feels to me like she has a poet standing over each shoulder: one who sounds very much like Edmond Jabès, whispering "Wandering creates the desert" into one ear; and the other, who sounds very much like Paul Celan, whispering into the other ear, "Reality is not simply there, it does not simply exist: it must be sought out and won." The notion that language, when applied to the world, creates and destroys the world—that it irredeemably stains the silence where the world might have been, the silence *that* the world might have been—feels central in Schwartz's (and Jabès's and Celan's) work broadly, but it feels particularly foregrounded in "*Blue.*"

Schwartz begins at the beginning, Genesis or something like it, antiquity certainly, "*wine-dark*" perhaps a nod to Homer's favorite marine epithet: "*once / we were // thrashing the sea / was wine-dark.*" And then: "*flash // of wing / and nothing / was the same.*" The unsameness caused by "*flash // of wing*" somehow numinous, ineluctable, and impossible to touch with language—"*nothing / was the same*" is all we get, only that broadest assertion. The poet (plenty capable of granular description elsewhere) illuminates the insufficiency of language for the task set before her by not even attempting an approach. This is no failure of Schwartz's lyric; it's a testament to her psychospiritual and lyric maturity. Again, Jabès: "Silence is no weakness of language. It is, on the contrary, its strength. It is the weakness of words not to know this."

"Blue" ends: "*what did // you lose / in becoming / family what // dazzling otherwise / do I name / when I // address you.*" The way the poem performs its skepticism of taxonomizing wonder, obstinately remaining on the side of its "*dazzling otherwise,*" feels so instructive to me, so lasting. The opportunity cost of a name is every other name, yes, but it's also namelessness.

THE ESTUARY

The brown bear living near the estuary,
and wading out when the tide swells and the salmon run,
during the days of the dwindling salmon runs,
and slapping with his big right paw a hook-nosed fish
whipsawing inland to spawn,
the ambidextrous bear,
furred like the forest from which he emerged,
waddling into the unteachable waters
to swat the salmon out the fast-running tide
and catch the red salmon in his mouth
and toss and juggle the sockeye salmon
thrashing and drowning in the air—
and when he's expressed himself completely
he catches with his jaw the self
that swam ten thousand miles to the estuary
and daintily, mincingly, with one paw grasping
the caudal fin and the other the head,
eats that salmon as if he were we
and the fish an ear of boiled corn—
that bear is a bear about whom rich and complicated
feelings can be felt. That is a bear from whom ideas
about the state of nature can be derived.
Cruelty is the wrong word to describe
the pleasure he gets from playing with his lunch.
Play and life are the same thing to him,
art and life, life and death.
Creation impinging on a consciousness
clear and crystalline. Pinpoint revelatory
explosions unsoiled by words, unbesmirched.

Creation clambering out of the waters,
shaking itself off, creation
surrounding itself with itself . . .
Stay down on the pavement where you just fell in a heap
like a bag of laundry, just stay there. Move even a
little and you might damage something else.
You've already done plenty of damage.
Stay down, supine. Stay down,
and let the giant buildings loom over you, let them
in their abstract imperium stun you with their indifference.
Wasn't that the reason you built them in the first place?
Stay down, stay down, and ask yourself:
"Could I be the bear in this fable?"
"Could I be the fish?"
"Could I be whoever is imagining all this?"

Susan Stewart on Vijay Seshadri's "The Estuary"

An estuary—a place of duality, where freshwater rivers meet the salt water of the sea. Snails, crabs, fish, seagrass, migratory birds all can flourish there, yet an estuary is a site where humans harvest but do not dwell.

Vijay Seshadri's "The Estuary" is a poem about a "brown bear living near the estuary" and as well a reflection upon the many meanings of "to take place": What does it mean to claim possession? Where are we along the path of evolution? How do we know an event has happened?

The bear is catching a salmon. The salmon are running in their thousand-mile journey from the sea to the gravel-based alpine streams—the exact spots—where each was born. There they will spawn and die. Later, their offspring will be carried by rivers to the sea, where they will live their own adult lives before making the same leaping journey back to their place of origin. Seshadri, a poet of exiles and returns, knows this world intimately, and here the tragic story of a vanished pair of salmon fishers told in his celebrated long poem "The Lump" finds its antithesis.

In the poem's opening lines, the word "salmon" recurs, incantatory. Noticing, matching, remembering nod to the perspective of the hunting bear as he catches his prey. Then "Cruelty is the wrong word to describe" how he plays with the salmon before abruptly eating it like "an ear of boiled corn." At this switch to a human metaphor, the spell of description breaks and the poem pivots to its enormous moral compass: "Play and life are the same thing to him, / art and life, life and death"; the place of human beings in creation: the possibility that our achievements are a mere display of indifference. In the end, we are left with the reciprocal trust the reader places in the poet, the poet in the reader, and the poet in himself—a trust rooted not in nature, but in the imagination.

I once fought the idea of the body as artifact,

my hair hanging long, romancing my waist. Down by the creek with
     my baby,
marsh marigolds slick as melted butter. His hair sticking up in small
     flames
like the choir-boy candles we dragged out of the mausoleum each
     December,

their wax mouths holding a pure note for decades. I was nebulous as
     an amoeba
or a nebula, hot water bottle with a flimsy skin, my clothes flowed,
     my eyes

changed color in the fall, my horse was made of rainwater. The key
to the transformation was eyeliner, eyeliner and a series of deaths.
     I began
to outline my eyes in kohl designed for the stage. Gold wristbands
     from

Woolworth's downtown and long, body-hugging shifts I designed
     and sewed
in Home Ec class, uneven seams, metallic thread. I cut bangs with
     pinking shears

and hardened my bob with Dippity-Do, my eyelashes fixed into
     black points
like the minute hand on my dead father's watch. I embarked on
     an affair
with my English teacher, a hairy man with a barrel chest who
     brought a bottle

of Cuervo in his briefcase to our house when my mother was at the
    gambling
boat. You think you're immortal, he said, but you're not. I'd learned how

to hold my face still, my whole body still, even when I waxed the
    big slide
at Kelly's Sportsland, two pieces of waxed paper under a burlap
    sack during
the lunar eclipse. I wore a lip gloss that made my mouth look like
    glass and rode

the frisky horse of time, mane braided with stars, down the
    serpentine humps
of the slide. A stone horse, but I was flying.

Erika L. Sánchez on Diane Seuss's "I once fought the idea of the body as artifact,"

Diane Seuss is a witch. I mean this as the highest form of praise. What I mean is that the spirit of the witch is so thick and vast that it cannot be shredded. Not in this world, not on the page, not in the great beyond . . . You get the idea. A woman with knowledge, and therefore, suspicious; a hazard to the flimsy-hearted.

"I once fought the idea of the body as artifact," is a poem that entrances me. I read it aloud again and again to my child and cat. Beauty is an altar and a pyre. It is everything and nothing all at once. The poem reveals the grotesqueness of gender and the violence of men. It rebukes notions of the female body as an object that is dead and studied. This poem is so alive that it overwhelms me. I can feel its pulse in my hands. The words knock around my body in the most pleasing way.

When I read the line "my horse was made of rainwater," I'm filled with awe and a sliver of longing. *I wish I had written that.* I nod/shake my head vigorously. The language of this poem tastes like an elegant vinegar. A vinegar infused with a hysterical sweetness. It's beautiful in its gaudiness, its playfulness, its acidity. Also, it's funny. Never have I ever read a phrase like "Dippity-Do." Not in a book or real life. But it delighted me in ways I still don't understand. It's almost too much, but then it's not too much, which is the point, right? It's the thing you need. A chilled Coke in the desert. This poem dances on the metaphorical blade. It does the jitterbug.

---

from "Personal Effects" by Solmaz Sharif
from *Look*

A young soldier (pictured above) the son of an imam, brother to six, is among the latest casualties in the military campaign of Susangerd.

Layli Long Soldier on Solmaz Sharif's "Personal Effects"

When I speak about documentary poetics, I turn to *Look*, written by Solmaz Sharif, which engages with the United States Department of Defense's *Dictionary of Military and Associated Terms*. Among the many powerful pieces within *Look*, one of my favorites is a poem about which I must first ask, can I call it a poem? Midway down the page, in italics, we see a single sentence. It is a caption to a photo. Sharif directs us to look above, to a photo that is noticeably absent. As I see it, this *absence*, then, is the poem. Because it leads us to ask: *Why* can't we see the photo? *Why* has Sharif chosen not to show us?

I cannot assume to know why, exactly, Sharif does not show the photograph. I can only speculate, admire, or simply relate and respond. My bodily response, the most truthful, is to relax. I relax, instinctually, in environments of safety and respect. For this reason, I regard this piece as a gesture of respect. Sharif does not display the image of the young soldier for the reader's consumption or spectacle. His image is private; and what is private, I believe, is sacred. This is an important point I share with my students, especially young Native writers: remember, you can *choose* what to share and what to withhold. And what you withhold may vibrate at a higher frequency than what's on the page. These choices are the poet's agency—or better yet, a form of *sovereignty*. Withholding is a way of saying, you cannot see this, know this, or take this; it's an assertion of immeasurable integrity.

In this one-sentence poem, Sharif has asked me to see without seeing. How does she do that? I realize now, *this* is the poem. In the absence of a photo I'm told is "pictured above," I have no choice, therefore, to view inwardly. I must contemplate / I must feel. Though I can't name the feeling, I can say with certainty, it sits right.

Jason Shinder
from *Stupid Hope*

ETERNITY

A poem written three thousand years ago

about a man who walks among horses
grazing on a hill under the small stars

comes to life on a page in a book

and the woman reading the poem,
in the silence between the words,

in her kitchen, filled, with a gold, metallic light,

finds the experience of living in that moment
so clearly described as to make her feel finally known

by someone. And every time the poem is read,

no matter her situation or her age,
this is more or less what happens.

Sophie Cabot Black on Jason Shinder's "Eternity"

"Eternity" was written for all of us: poem lovers, poets, soul artists, those who pay attention, those who want to pay attention. This poem holds everything essential in its two capable hands: words about words and word-making; a man, a woman, a horse, a hill, stars, a bound book, a kitchen, a table. Life again; even after, even before. Silence and space, time folding in on itself; Jason Shinder uses these cosmic forces magnificently in his work, deceptively simple, yet eternal. This is a poem with centrifugal force, engendering itself, urging everything around it (and within it) to organize, and yet remain human and humane.

Shinder approached poetry from all angles, daring us into reading what we are not familiar with, to read, write, gather, and form communities where we all might experience together. He was a poet of inclusion and believed in every perspective a poem could be written from; as he would often remind us, especially when some of us got cranky with the world of mediocrity: there is room for us all. Shinder embodied so much: he was born a poet, deeply noticing, while also suffering, the world. He was also an activist, a promoter, a teacher, an enabler, and an entrepreneur.

Poems are ultimately about poetry and this poem is no exception. To stay close to the place that brought you here is the poet's domain. The generative moment, to try and remember the why. Shinder asks us, brings us, back to this place. The reader, the poet, the poem, the woman: all transformed, validated, known.

Danez Smith
from *Homie*

GAY CANCER

     Melvin, Assotto, Essex, my Saint
Laurent, Xtravaganza House of
      sissy & boosted silk   dirt throned
with your too soon   it grew
           in me too   blood's gossip
  cum cussed   gifted to us
     from us   yes   it grows by the day
still   i'm sorry we are still in the midst
of ourselves here   a pill for your grave
    a door to our later years
you deserved   o mother o sweet unc
   who we miss & never knew
                 is that you?
    my wrist to my ear
          you're here

Carl Phillips on Danez Smith's "gay cancer"

I love teaching Danez Smith's "gay cancer" as an example of homage in poetry, of how contradiction can be a prosodic device, and for its logic of resistance. The poem opens with homage: to Melvin Dixon, Assotto Saint, and Essex Hemphill, the three patron saints of gay male poetry, three of the earliest to write openly about queer Black male sex, and to die of AIDS, called "gay cancer" before anyone really knew what AIDS was. Homage as well to drag's celebration of excess, camp, sex, fashion, joy, represented here by Yves Saint Laurent and the most famous house in the NYC underground ballroom scene, the House of Xtravaganza.

Meanwhile, contradiction begins at the title, if we read gay as "happy," and if we agree that cancer is nothing to be happy about. Contradiction turns out to be a patterning device for Smith's poem: the ordinariness of dirt beside the royalty of a throne; the conflation of curse and gift in "cum cussed   gifted to us"; the pill that extends life side by side with the grave holding those who died before pills had been developed; the contradiction of missing those whom we "never knew."

(Meanwhile, steady but unpredictable rhymes throughout, tempering contradiction with sonic agreement . . .)

The poem enacts and is shaped by the particular conundrum of being queer, Black, and HIV-positive, of being more keenly and daily aware than others of one's mortality because of these parts of who one is. The conundrum, too, of feeling distant from the dead and yet so intimate with them that all one has to do is lift a wrist to the ear to hear them, feel them, in our pulse, that sign of life still happening—by which logic, how are the dead truly dead?

And isn't this the slyest sonnet ever?

———————————————

Tracy K. Smith

from *Such Color: New and Selected Poems*

BEE ON A SILL

Submits to its own weight,
the bulb of itself too full,

too weak or too wise
to lift and go.

And something blunt in me
remembers the old charade

about putting a thing out
of its misery. For it? For me?

Sleep, Bee, deep and easy.
Hive, heave, give, grieve.

Then rise when you're ready
from your soul's hard floor

to sweet work
or some war.

Courtney Faye Taylor on Tracy K. Smith's "Bee on a Sill"

Reading Tracy K. Smith's "Bee on a Sill," I consider the space between those who hold power and those who thrive despite that power. In an insect, I see my marginality. In a contemplative speaker, I see my capability. To be both identities is to be both vulnerable and complicit, a duality that captures the shape of the human condition.

"Bee on a Sill" is a direct descendant of Lucille Clifton's "cruelty. don't talk to me about cruelty." Both ponder the choice to spare or destroy, to empathize or self-center. Clifton shows the ruthless decision; a broom slices through a country of roaches. Smith stops short of that image. The bee survives. Violence is hushed to make a case for grace.

Employing a severe gentleness, Smith sings the truth of precarity, of possibility. Here, I'm reminded of our most pressing desire: freedom—the freedom to "Hive, heave, give, grieve. // Then rise." To be the recipient of that freedom. To be the granter of it.

VITA

God guided my hand
and it wrote,
"Forget my name."

World, please note—
a life went by, just
a life, no claims,

A stutter in the millions
of stars that pass,
a voice that lulled—

A glance
and a world
and a hand.

Jim Moore on William Stafford's "Vita"

It's not unsurprising that Willam Stafford would include, in a poem called "Vita," the line "Forget my name." "No claims," he says in the poem, but, there is, in fact, this claim: that a poem can help a reader find their way in our unlikely and unnerving universe. "Vita" serves as a coda—at once both offhand and mysterious—to a life devoted to poetry, day after day and decade after decade. Poetry was a life-work for Stafford, and he served it up to, and including, the day that he died.

Stafford was one of the first poets whose work I loved when I began writing poetry more than fifty years ago. How lucky I was to stumble across his poems back then! And how miraculous that I need his poems as much today as then: especially his willingness to let himself be thrown off-balance within the writing of the poem, just as we are so often thrown off-balance in the living of our lives. He trusts the poem to let it take him where he needs to go. "Vita," of course, means "life," in Italian, from the Latin. His poems have been life lessons from the first, for me: friends along the way. But the kinds of friends who challenge as well as comfort.

These twelve lines make many of the moves that mark a Stafford poem, especially the way he feints away from an expected word or phrase and instead finds something stranger, cagier, more open to bewilderment and amazement. That *glance* in the last stanza, that *world*, that *hand*: the whole poem is an invitation to remember just how terrifying and magnificent it is to live among "the millions / of stars that pass."

Don't lose heart, I sometimes remind myself: *remember Stafford*.

Susan Stewart

from *Cinder: New and Selected Poems*

THE FOREST

You should lie down now and remember the forest,
for it is disappearing—
no, the truth is it is gone now
and so what details you can bring back
might have a kind of life.

Not the one you had hoped for, but a life
—you should lie down now and remember the forest—
nonetheless, you might call it "in the forest,"
no the truth is, it is gone now,
starting somewhere near the beginning, that edge,

Or instead the first layer, the place you remember
(not the one you had hoped for, but a life)
as if it were firm, underfoot, for that place is a sea,
nonetheless, you might call it "in the forest,"
which we can never drift above, we were there or we were not,

No surface, skimming. And blank in life, too,
or instead the first layer, the place you remember,
as layers fold in time, black humus there,
as if it were firm, underfoot, for that place is a sea,
like a light left hand descending, always on the same keys.

The flecked birds of the forest sing behind and before
no surface, skimming. And blank in life, too,
sing without a music where there cannot be an order,
as layers fold in time, black humus there,
where wide swatches of light slice between gray trunks,

Where the air has a texture of drying moss,
the flecked birds of the forest sing behind and before:
a musk from the mushrooms and scalloped molds.
They sing without a music where there cannot be an order,
though high in the dry leaves something does fall,

Nothing comes down to us here.
Where the air has a texture of drying moss,
(in that place where I was raised) the forest was tangled,
a musk from the mushrooms and scalloped molds,
tangled with brambles, soft-starred and moving, ferns

And the marred twines of cinquefoil, false strawberry, sumac—
nothing comes down to us here,
stained. A low branch swinging above a brook
in that place where I was raised, the forest was tangled,
and a cave just the width of shoulder blades.

You can understand what I am doing when I think of the entry—
and the marred twines of cinquefoil, false strawberry, sumac—
as a kind of limit. Sometimes I imagine us walking there
(. . . pokeberry, stained. A low branch swinging above a brook)
in a place that is something like a forest.

But perhaps the other kind, where the ground is covered
(you can understand what I am doing when I think of the entry)
by pliant green needles, there below the piney fronds,
a kind of limit. Sometimes I imagine us walking there.
And quickening below lie the sharp brown blades,

The disfiguring blackness, then the bulbed phosphorescence of the roots.
But perhaps the other kind, where the ground is covered,
so strangely alike and yet singular, too, below
the pliant green needles, the piney fronds.
Once we were lost in the forest, *so strangely alike and yet singular, too,*
but the truth is, it is, lost to us now.

Jennifer Grotz on Susan Stewart's "The Forest"

Susan Stewart's "The Forest" has haunted me now for nearly thirty years. An accompanying endnote states the poem is for Polish journalist Ryszard Kapuściński who, Stewart writes, "suggested to me that a time may come when no one will remember the experience of a forest." A chilling thought, one we all live with still, and chilling to think awareness of this particular manifestation of "the end of nature" (remembering Bill McKibben's foundational book first appeared in 1989) has been hovering in our consciousness for most of my life. I recently discovered that "endling," surely the saddest word in the English language, was coined soon after, in the April 4, 1996, issue of *Nature* magazine, denoting the last living individual in a species.

"The Forest" reads as incantation, as spell, revering the forest by recreating its wildness in its own form. Stewart sends us into memory, into dream, in unforgettable ways, from the beginning: "You should lie down now and remember the forest." In what I understand to be a nonce form, the poem's composed of eleven stanzas, the first ten of which are five lines long and each repeat two lines from the previous stanza (lines two and four) while introducing three new lines (lines one, three, and five). A six-line envoi stanza repeats lines from itself *"so strangely alike and yet singular, too"* as well as the poem's beginning. Resembling a sort of reverse pantoum, the poem weaves a mesmerizing reading experience of simultaneous familiarity and disorientation, of being "tangled" and, in the end, "lost" in the forest—and lost in the forest of the poem, too.

THE TROUBADOURS ETC.

Just for this evening, let's not mock them.
Not their curtsies or cross-garters
or ever-recurring pepper trees in their gardens
promising, promising.

At least they had ideas about love.

All day we've driven past cornfields, past cows poking their heads
through metal contraptions to eat.
We've followed West 84, and what else?
Irrigation sprinklers fly past us, huge wooden spools in the fields,
lounging sheep, telephone wires,
yellowing flowering shrubs.

Before us, above us, the clouds swell, layers of them,
the violet underneath of clouds.
Every idea I have is nostalgia. Look up:
there is the sky that passenger pigeons darkened and filled—
darkened for days, eclipsing sun, eclipsing all other sound
with the thunder of their wings.
After a while, it must have seemed that they followed
not instinct or pattern but only
one another.

When they stopped, Audubon observed,
they broke the limbs of stout trees by the weight of the numbers.

And when we stop we'll follow—what?
Our *hearts*?

The Puritans thought that we are granted the ability to love
only through miracle,
but the troubadours knew how to burn themselves through,
how to make themselves shrines to their own longing.
The spectacular was never behind them.

Think of days of those scarlet-breasted, blue-winged birds above you.
Think of me in the garden, humming
quietly to myself in my blue dress,
a blue darker than the sky above us, a blue dark enough for storms,
though cloudless.

At what point is something gone completely?
The last of the sunlight is disappearing
even as it swells—

Just for this evening, won't you put me before you
until I'm far enough away you can
believe in me?

Then try, try to come closer—
my wonderful and less than.

Natalie Diaz on Mary Szybist's "The Troubadours Etc."

Mary Szybist's "The Troubadours Etc." urges me to accept the gift of poetry as not just art or story, but as a practice of living a life toward love, whether love comes or not, stays or goes, breaks the bough or burns through the clouds. "Let's not mock them," Szybist says of the troubadours, who dared moments of love and joy, in the midst of love's larger absences.

The work of the poet is not unlike the work of the troubadours: There is an emotional toll in seeking language for the inexplicable, the songs of feeling. There is a price for looking into the interior of the self. So too, the work of prayer—to ask of the light for more light. Or the work of the lover—to bloom or thorn in the ecstatic agony of electrons between their own hand and the hand of their lover. Too, the work of the dreamer and even the dream itself—making the ordinary strange. It is a durational labor, looking closely, intentionally and attentively, until what we knew becomes unknown, and we become curious again, desirous again, afraid again, and therefore sensually alert and capable of relearning the world with self-tenderness and *in consequence* to one another. Nabokov called it "a momentary vacuum into which rushes all that I love. A sense of oneness with sun and stone."

We cannot write what is *gone* back into nostalgic presence—we killed to extinction the passenger pigeon, among others. Szybist instead enters the absence, setting it in front of us, not behind us, as feeling, a generative practice of the world we are creating. In this poem, absence is the distance required in all desire. The final lines remind me of the necessary work of wonder—to put the world, my beloveds, my brother, my desert, my river, before me with such devotion that we are nothing less than miracles, and in seeing ourselves as spectacular, we are prepared to speak or sing love into an unreasonable world.

Courtney Faye Taylor
from *Concentrate*

So far my sentence as a Black woman has been   hard to hone,
homed in sore white pith. Put graciously, Black womanhood has been
a limb that's fallen asleep beneath me, paddy wagon of spinal cords
in Baltimore's traffic up ahead. This whole color was a mistake—a
leak in the ceiling whorehouse, a confused ass whooping. You see the
baby in the blinds, the eager run in nylons, a public school lisp making
room for the velour of her name. I was one of them. In grade school.
It seemed my whole class had fallen asleep in front of a microwave. I
drew faces on my galas then ate them off. God to me was my distantly
gentle Aunt Notrie; brilliant completely, Virginia Slims and bread-
sticks, the shade on her side of Brewster slouched the coolish way a
suburb deserves. Sunday, she was an usher with one breast. I crept
to mom 'n' pops where bells above doors snitched to mention my en-
trance. But I tolled them bells. I was toys to be bothered. I had made
such toyish mistakes. In any Black sentence, you'd love nothing more
than to had made   no mistake.

Malcolm Tariq on Courtney Faye Taylor's "So far"

Upon first reading "So far," the poem that opens Courtney Faye Taylor's *Concentrate*, mentions of a "Black sentence" holding the poem at both ends become apparent almost immediately. Her use of a prosaic structure reads almost as if the speaker is writing her own life history or delivering a testimony amid a legal sentencing. More keenly, Taylor's language throughout yields image upon image. Each sentence builds on what was previously laid out for it, stacking visual markers, descriptions, and actions.

"So far" is a bold opening in the way that it invites you to look but not touch. There is no breaking the speaker's truth here. For poetry about Black women and girls, this is key. It is also a powerful assertion of self and a necessary taking of space rarely extended to them. Like so much of Taylor's work, the voice is deliberate, cradling a complexity as deep as Blackness. The speaker in this poem begins with the personal. Only when she offers a bit of distance does she ring the reader's line: "You see the baby in the blinds, the eager run in nylons, a public school lisp making room for the velour of her name. I was one of them. In grade school." That "you" is no passive rendering. True to Taylor's poetic practice, what's personal is always political. The reader must be invoked, called upon to not only witness but question. We don't know which bears more weight, the "you" or the "I." This is haunting work. And necessary.

In her writings about Black girlhood, Taylor's work is the concentrated matter invoked by Gwendolyn Brooks when she says, "Poetry is life distilled. Life is not always nice or proper or happy or smooth or even-edged." This is what I am constantly learning from "So far" and all the poems after it in *Concentrate*—to get to the root of the thing. Then to the root of that root. And hold it.

———————————————

Tomas Tranströmer
translated from the Swedish by Robert Bly
from *The Half-Finished Heaven: Selected Poems*

FROM AN AFRICAN DIARY (1963)

In the painting of the kitsch Congolese artists
the figures are skinny as insects, their human energy saddened.
The road from one way of life to another is hard.
The one who has arrived has a long way to go.

A young African found a tourist lost among the huts.
He couldn't decide whether to make him a friend or object of blackmail.
The indecision upset him. They parted in confusion.

Europeans stick near their cars as if the cars were Mama.
Cicadas are strong as electric razors. The cars drive home.
Soon the lovely darkness comes and washes the dirty clothes. Sleep.
The one who has arrived has a long way to go.

Perhaps a migratory flock of handshakes would help.
Perhaps letting the truth escape from books would help.
We have to go farther.

The student studies all night, studies and studies so he can be free.
When the examination is over, he turns into a stair-rung for the next man.
A hard road.
The one who has arrived has a long way to go.

Vijay Seshadri on Tomas Tranströmer's "From an African Diary (1963)," translated from the Swedish by Robert Bly

I've been reading "From an African Diary (1963)" for almost all its life in English. Over the years, the poem has changed in the way all great art changes as its beholders change, but also changed in ways that only this poem can change.

"From an African Diary (1963)" has the distance and dimension and silence, the vast inner landscape, that characterize Tomas Tranströmer's poetry. It also has a fixed location in Africa; a time stamp, 1963. Together these call up a tragic postcolonial circumstance. The Congo, exploited by the Belgians for almost a century, newly emerged as the Democratic Republic of the Congo, has become trapped in Cold War power politics and civil war, and has seen its first prime minister, the pan-Africanist progressive Patrice Lumumba, assassinated in 1961 through the connivance of Western powers and their African clients.

Tranströmer's sympathies are obvious, but his twilit, hyperborean sensibility and his imaginative restraint keep these facts on the other side of the poem. Their presence becomes structural (and all the more powerful for that). They exert a gravitational pressure that binds, unifies, and fuses a complex symbolic action, an action involving race and racial asymmetry, detachment and involvement, cultures in collision, paradoxical refrains, grief. "The one who has arrived has a long way to go."

For decades, I read this poem as it asked me to. I followed it to its existential conclusion—the student at the end stands in, unconditionally, for all the actors in the drama: the African and the European, the speaker, the poet, the reader, the invisible Lumumba. The poem, as Tranströmer meant it to, resolves in universality. Today, it's impossible not to notice the privilege of the speaker, acknowledged in the poem but never foregrounded. What does our contemporary recognition of this privilege do for the poem? I would say that it deepens it immeasurably, that the poem has evolved as we have evolved, and still remains ahead of us, close but just out of reach.

Natasha Trethewey
from *Bellocq's Ophelia*

JANUARY 1911

I know you are driven
to such harsh words
first, out of your concern
for me, and second,
out of your gentle piousness
which I still fondly recall—
the modest tilt of your head,
even when you scolded me,
your prayer book tucked
neatly between the cushions
of your settee. My dear,

please do not think
I am the wayward girl
you describe. I alone
have made this choice.
Save what I pay for board,
what I earn is mine. Now
my labor is my own.
Already my purse swells.
I have bought my mother
some teeth, paid to have
her new well dug. Perhaps

you are too delicate to know
of my life here. Still,
you remain my dearest friend
and should not worry
that I won't write. I know

your own simple means
prevent you from helping me
as you would like. Help me only
as you already do—with the words
I crave, the mundane details
of your quiet life.

Donika Kelly on Natasha Trethewey's "January 1911"

I encountered "January 1911" from Natasha Trethewey's *Bellocq's Ophelia* when I was a graduate student trying to figure out what kind of poet I wanted to be. I'd already fallen in love with Trethewey's later work for its clarity and music, her deft use of closed form as a container for enormous feeling, but *Bellocq's Ophelia*, and this poem in particular, was a revelation.

Ophelia, the protagonist of the collection, is an imagined character, "a prostitute photographed circa 1912 by E. J. Bellocq, later collected in the book, *Storyville Portraits*." This epistolary poem, a poem in the form of a letter, is Ophelia's response to her former teacher, Constance, who is concerned about Ophelia's decision to become a sex worker.

"January 1911" taught me about the power of line breaks and stanza breaks to show feeling. Ophelia has made her decision, and while that's a complicated choice, it's not one she cares to have questioned. So, the lines are terse but also careful: terse because it's her choice, but careful because she loves Constance. Most lines end with nouns or verbs, anchoring the poem in memory, the objects and the act of recollection. She is calling Constance to mind, carefully, picking her way through feeling.

My favorite part is the end of the first stanza. You can almost hear the deep breath she must take at the end of the first stanza—"My dear," she says. Comma. Line break. Stanza break. I gasped the first time I got to this moment in the poem. I would love to write a line, to turn it so skillfully, to allow my speaker that extra beat. The theater of it! Here is the hand of the poet showing us the mind of the speaker. This is the space of composition, of Ophelia composing herself for Constance quite literally in the act of writing a letter. But she is also composing herself emotionally, so that she can remember her friend.

Mai Der Vang
From *Afterland*

AFTER ALL HAVE GONE

I once carried my mollusk tune
All the way to the lottery of gods.

Rain was the old funeral choir
That keened of a hemisphere

Moored under lampwings.
Clouds never left. I knew

The lights would shine clearer
If I closed my eyes, just as

I knew the Pacific would teach
Me to sleep before tying my

Name to the flaming. Here I
Am now at the end of amethyst,

Drizzling another lost sunrise
Inside the quilt of my hand.

Tarfia Faizullah on Mai Der Vang's "After All Have Gone"

In the near middle of Mai Der Vang's *Afterland* is a poem I keep reread-
ing aloud. The title's temporality caught my eye first, how it pitches
time both forward to a possibly distant future, as well as backward to-
ward a recent past. The title also connects me to aloneness—but not
necessarily loneliness. How many times have I dreaded that everyone
would disappear, and how many times have I waited to be alone (ex-
quisitely, indulgently)? Oh, the profound quiet after the party is over
and the guests have all gone! Ah, the way we are all infinitely together,
and alone.

The poem itself conjures images and objects that feel ancient: a
mollusk, a funeral choir, the "lottery of gods," an amethyst, a quilt.
These objects/symbols are situated inside of incredibly vast natural
spaces: the hemisphere, the Pacific, clouds, a sunrise, "the flaming."
This juxtaposition of ancient objects described amid the natural world
results in an arresting poem that is also, somehow, a vivid painting.

Before I, too, like the "All" in the title, go, I must spotlight one
specific enjambment. At the end of the first line of the second-to-last
stanza is this lovely little "Here I." Two small monosyllabic words that
are also huge concepts. I love this poet's decision to end a line on the
word "I"—and the effect is far from solipsistic. The "All" in the title
and the "I" close to the end of this poem seem to be connected, though
there is almost a whole poem that separates them. No matter if there
is an "All" that goes, Vang's poem seems to be saying, there is still such
a thing as "Here." There is still such a thing as the eye.

James L. White
from *The Salt Ecstasies*

MAKING LOVE TO MYSELF

When I do it, I remember how it was with us.
Then my hands remember too,
and you're with me again, just the way it was.

After work when you'd come in and
turn the TV off and sit on the edge of the bed,
filling the room with gasoline smell from your overalls,
trying not to wake me which you always did.
I'd breathe out long and say,
'Hi Jess, you tired baby?'
You'd say not so bad and rub my belly,
not after me really, just being sweet,
and I always thought I'd die a little
because you smelt like burnt leaves or woodsmoke.

We were poor as Job's turkey but we lived well—
the food, a few good movies, good dope, lots of talk,
lots of you and me trying on each other's skin.

What a sweet gift this is,
done with my memory, my cock and hands.

Sometimes I'd wake up wondering if I should fix
coffee for us before work,
almost thinking you're here again, almost seeing
your work jacket on the chair.

I wonder if you remember what
we promised when you took the job in Laramie?
Our way of staying with each other.
We promised there'd always be times
when the sky was perfectly lucid,
that we could remember each other through that.
You could remember me at my worktable
or in the all-night diners,
though we'd never call or write.

I just have to stop here Jess.
I just have to stop.

Eduardo C. Corral on James L. White's "Making Love to Myself"

There are two sets of poets vital to an emerging poet's writing practice. The first set is recommended by a writing instructor. These poets welcome the newer poet onto the page, to the possibilities dwelling inside language. The second set is discovered by the poet. These poets complicate assumptions about languages, forms, and canons. James L. White, for me, belongs to the second set. I discovered, in the late 1990s, *The Salt Ecstasies* on a shelf at Hayden Library at Arizona State University. The title caught my attention. How it elevated salt to the realm of desire. The speaker's vulnerability, queerness, and struggles with money and weight resonated with me, and I particularly felt a kinship with "Making Love to Myself."

The poem begins with a tercet, three lines, an uneven number. Because of this unevenness, the eye moves to the next stanza in search of balance. The tercet is crowded with the speaker, the titular action, the hands, the "us," the "you," and the past. I love how the tercet pushes the reader through the overwhelming rush of a blossoming memory. The second stanza is composed of ten lines, which allows the reader to dwell on the bittersweet memory: the speaker and Jess softly talking on a bed. The poem concludes with a couplet—a narrow room. The speaker declares he doesn't want to continue, but his last words linger, echo.

There's a progression of aromas in the second stanza. In the third line, the "gasoline smell from your overalls" begins to surge though the room. Gasoline is man-made and offensive to the nose. But the smells rising from Jess's body are rooted in the natural world. He smells like "burnt leaves" and "woodsmoke." The leaves and wood are on fire. But when in our history has homosexuality ever been safe? The conflating of the dangerous and the pleasurable is queer. The queerness in White's work was and is a refuge.

LENT

I saw the jaundiced fist of rhubarb
punch through the February crust

there in the corner bed where I spread
the wood ashes. Its crenellations

tendered through mud and grit.
A bit of leaf-mold crowned it.

The cardinal sweet-sang
to the elongated day

from behind his night-black mask.
The woods graying still,

a forest of beams. Cold tamps sap
back down the taproot.

The titmouse pips a seed hull.
The cherry swells a node

of red and the hive stokes
the chip of sun that is their queen.

Three months back the world
was undone, flesh starved

to sinew. We spent our days
swaddled in wool and down,

banking the plate-stove with cedar
to remake summer's heat

on our outstretched hands.
The night sent up a tallow disk

and constellations bridged
the unknowable. We chose our meals

from among the globes of fruit
sweetened under glass in the pantry.

Look now as the world swims back.
Down the road reddish lambs

butt heads, nurse the swelled bag
of their dam. By the road, the remains

of a fox appear as the gray
snow peels back, recoiling

from the sun.
A bit of wind

noses the fur, as I pick
the skull to prop atop the stone wall.

Does the vixen sleep
alone in her den? Will she whelp

another litter of kits,
or will she keep her face

tucked in the stole of her tail
and rot away the summer

soundless but for
the blowfly's repetition

as it transports her portion bit by bit
into the warming sky?

Gretchen Marquette on Mark Wunderlich's "Lent"

In Mark Wunderlich's poems, nature is never infantilized or turned wholesale into metaphor—some potent facet of itself always remains, resilient and untouched. In the poem "Lent," spring is not allowed to become a shorthand for heralding new life. In the realm of this poem, people are "swaddled in wool and down," and choosing "meals / from among the globes of fruit / sweetened under glass in the pantry," while the wild world "tamps sap / back down the taproot." There is a kind of submission to winter that has taken place in both human and nonhuman animals, and spring arrives as a potential disturbance to this rest, an almost unnecessary relief brought to a weary, but well-prepared world. "Does the vixen sleep / alone in her den?" he asks. "Will she whelp // another litter of kits, / or will she keep her face // tucked in the stole of her tail / and rot away the summer . . . ?" The answer might be that it doesn't matter either way.

What matters is that the relentlessness and—from a human perspective—cruelty of the natural world is belied by its great durability. We can admire, and live inside this durable world, uncomfortable as it may be for us, and begin our life's work of accepting that while the same world that holds us will never see us as valuable individuals, we will remain, even after death, necessary components in an intricate system. "A bit of wind // noses the fur, as I pick / the skull to prop atop the stone wall," writes Wunderlich, acknowledging the agency we have, in our daily lives and in our work, to acknowledge one another. In this we find a grim and gracious peace.

Jenny Xie
  from *Eye Level*

ONGOING

Never mind the distances traveled, the companion
she made of herself. The threadbare twenties not
to be underestimated. A wild depression that ripped
from January into April. And still she sprouts an appetite.
Insisting on edges and cores, when there were none.
Relationships annealed through shared ambivalences.
Pages that steadied her. Books that prowled her
until the hard daybreak, and for months after.
Separating new vows from the old, like laundry whites.
Small losses jammed together so as to gather mass.
Stored generations of filtered quietude.
And some stubbornness. Tangles along the way
the comb-teeth of the mind had to bite through, but for what.
She had trained herself to look for answers at eye level,
but they were lower, they were changing all the time.

Kemi Alabi on Jenny Xie's "Ongoing"

I don't want poetry to order disorder. Most days, I want the mess of life on full display. Then there are days when I flail for poems like they're footholds in the abyss. The steadiest pages subvert my impulse to pit chaos and order against each other. Instead, they're revealed to be the two-headed desire of life itself. That's why I've held on to Jenny Xie's "Ongoing"—writing it longhand, memorizing lines. Through its chronicled stumbles, I trip out of the war I trained for, flopping back to wonder.

On one hand, it's wrong to call these fifteen lines an epic poem. On the other, maybe a millennial epic is more mood than length. On one hand, "Never mind the distances traveled." On the other, note the ripping and sprouting and prowling and biting and and and. Here's what's separated. Here's what's jammed together. Here's struggle's reward: more struggle. Here's the joke: it's all setup. Here's the nothing where the core should be.

The speaker reports the antihero's roaming with a clarity so precise, it must be hindsight. End-stopped lines emphasize the thudding dead ends. A favorite moment is line thirteen closing with, "but for what." Period. Not a real question, answers abandoned as ill-conceived tasks. The poem is a cautionary tale, and the speaker knows better—which is different from *doing* better, I'm told. But let's hope, at some point, the mind exhausts itself, giving in to what only the body knows. Narrative yielding to what only the lyric reveals. The journey still in motion, but complete enough for past tense. Not through some grand arrival, but surrender as simple as a tilt of the head.

Yi Lei

translated from the Chinese by Tracy K. Smith and Changtai Bi
from *My Name Will Grow Wide Like a Tree: Selected Poems*

BETWEEN STRANGERS

Stranger, who can measure the distance between us?
Distance is the rumor of a never-before-seen sea.
Distance the width of a layer of dust.
Maybe we need only strike a match
for my world to flicker in your sky,
Visible finally, and eye-to-eye.
Breachable, finally, the border between us.
What if we touched? What then?
Would something in us hum an old familiar song?
Maybe then our feet would wear a path back and forth
between our lives, like houses in neighboring lots.
Would you give me what I lack? Your winter coat,
Your favorite battered pot? Logic warns: unlikely.
History tells me to guard my distance
When I pass you on the street, and I obey.
But—to stumble into you, or you into me—
Wouldn't it be sweet? In reality,

I keep to myself. You keep to you. We have nothing
To rue. So why does remorse rise almost to my brim,
And also in you?

1985

Jenny Xie on Yi Lei's "Between Strangers," translated from the Chinese by Tracy K. Smith and Changtai Bi

Lost in translation: to leave one's mooring in the endless distances between two languages, and necessarily, those endless distances between two strangers. Lost, which is to say destabilized, in that migratory act, moving from one linguistic and cultural territory into another, into profound otherness. Smuggling the unsayable across borders.

Yi Lei was singular: one of China's most independent poets, renowned for her poems' transgressive erotic charge, pointed political critiques, and a boldness of spirit that cut through a patriarchal cultural order known for muffling voices like hers. The work was unapologetically frank. Her poems erupted into the post-Mao literary landscape during an era when her contemporaries—mostly male—wrote in an imagery-laden, highly elliptical style. Yi Lei's voice startled in its liberatory force and limpid self-announcement.

I found my way to Yi Lei's poems through Tracy K. Smith, a poet in whose work I feel indescribably found. Smith met Yi Lei by happenstance, over a Chinese New Year lunch in Manhattan. Neither spoke one another's language. Two strangers, yet as Smith describes it, undeniably pulled toward each other's orbit. Over the course of many years, alongside translator Changtai Bi—who translates from Mandarin—Smith would coax many of Yi Lei's poems into English, injecting them with her own rich rhythms and music, in an act of generous and ravishing collaboration. Across the translated poems, we detect the scent of the self's many others.

"Between Strangers" is a poem of doubled intimacies: of that described between strangers, and of that between the author and the translator, in dynamic dialogue. Two remarkable poets of our time: one from China, one from the United States. They meet on the page. Intimacy is what rises in the between, in the distance.

HANGMAN'S TREE

> *Yggdrasil*

To see a living thing—
a badly damaged
thing—and to fail

to understand
how life still catches
hold of it and clings

without falling through,
like water falling
through a bowl

more fissure than bowl.
Just as a bowl
must be waterproof,

a body must be
lifeproof, we assume,
as if a life were bound

by laws of gravity,
always seeking
a downward escape.

But then there is
this olive tree—
if *tree* is still

the word to describe
this improbable
arrangement

of bark and twig
and leaf—this tree
ripped in three pieces

down to the ground.
No longer a column,
instead a triple

helix of spiraling
bark verticals
sketching the outline

where the tree
used to be. No heartwood,
very little wood

left at all, the exposed
surfaces green
with moss, dandelions

filling the foot-wide
gap at its base. And still
the tree thrives,

taking its place
in the formal allée
that edges this gravel road,

sending out leafy shoots
and unripe olives
in the prescribed shapes

and quantities.
Lizard haven, beetle
home. I was wrong

when I told you
life starts at the center
and radiates outward.

There is another
mode of life, one
that draws sustenance

from the peripheries:
each slim leaf
slots itself

into the green air;
each capillary root
sutures itself

into the soil.
Together these
small adhesions

can bear the much-
diminished weight
of the whole.

I won't lie.
It will hurt.
It will force you

to depend on those
contingent things
you have always

professed to despise.
But it will suffice.
It will keep you alive.

Stephanie Burt on Monica Youn's "Hangman's Tree"

Many of us get told, or tell ourselves, we will find all the desiderata of bourgeois life if we only stay within the lines or else dare to cross them; if we take chances, or else do what we're told. We will end up beloved, comfortable, secured, and centered by the time we are thirty, or forty, if we only make the right choices, and if we don't, we must have chosen wrong.

That's what the late critic Lauren Berlant called cruel optimism. It's everywhere, and it's one of the major targets in Monica Youn's *Blackacre*, whose long skinny forms, complexly subordinated sentences, and usually short lines (though she also excels in prose poems) try hard to face facts that will always be hard to face. Most of us don't get most of the things that we want. Most of us don't get the things that our society tells us that we ought to want. Many get neither, and we punish ourselves, the way a tree, in Youn's world, might punish itself for not growing, or for putting out leaves but never flowers and seeds (much of *Blackacre* concerns infertility). "There is," she tells us hauntingly, with echoes of Marianne Moore's great "The Fish," "another / mode of life, one / that draws sustenance" from what cannot make it look young, or healthy, or obviously whole. But it is whole: we are whole, in a sense, as long as we can find the "contingent things" that demanding, ambitious, idealistic poets (I'm not one) "professed to despise."

"Hangman's Tree" is, inter alia, a way to describe a real tree, apparently an olive, a "triple / helix" split by lightning, disease or human violence, drought-tolerant, "exposed / surfaces green / with moss" at the edge of a "formal allée." Youn stands out, as usual, for her descriptive virtuosity. But she's also recommending a second- or a fourth-choice way of life that might turn out to be best for her, or me, or you: a way of life that does not depend on one love, one home, one culturally sanctified source of meaning or joy.

Kaveh Akbar is the author of two poetry collections, *Pilgrim Bell* and *Calling a Wolf a Wolf*, and a novel, *Martyr!* He is the poetry editor of the *Nation* and teaches at the University of Iowa.

Kemi Alabi is the author of *Against Heaven*, which was selected by Claudia Rankine for the Academy of American Poets First Book Award, and a coeditor of *The Echoing Ida Collection*.

Elizabeth Alexander is the author of several books of poetry, including *Crave Radiance: New and Selected Poems*. She delivered her poem "Praise Song for the Day" at the inauguration of President Barack Obama. She is the president of the Mellon Foundation.

Threa Almontaser is the author of *The Wild Fox of Yemen*, which was selected by Harryette Mullen for the Walt Whitman Award of the Academy of American Poets.

Mary Jo Bang has published numerous poetry collections, including *A Film in Which I Play Everyone* and *Elegy*, winner of the National Book Critics Circle Award.

Catherine Barnett is the author of several poetry collections, including *Solutions to the Problem of Bodies in Space, Human Hours*, and *The Game of Boxes*, winner of the James Laughlin Award of the Academy of American Poets.

Changtai Bi is cotranslator, with Tracy K. Smith, of *My Name Will Grow Wide Like a Tree* by Yi Lei.

Sophie Cabot Black is the author of the poetry collections *The Exchange, The Descent*, and *The Misunderstanding of Nature*, winner of the Norma Farber First Book Award.

Robert Bly (1926–2021) was a poet, essayist, and translator, the author of many books, including *The Light around the Body*, winner of the National Book Award. He is the translator of *The Half-Finished Heaven* by Nobel Prize winner Tomas Tranströmer, and *Airmail: The Letters of Robert Bly and Tomas Tranströmer* collects their correspondence.

Stephanie Burt is the author of several works of poetry and literary criticism, including *We Are Mermaids*, *Advice from the Lights*, and *Close Calls with Nonsense*, a finalist for the National Book Critics Circle Award. She teaches at Harvard University.

Eduardo C. Corral is the author of *Guillotine*, which was longlisted for the National Book Award, and *Slow Lightning*, winner of the Yale Poets Series.

Natalie Diaz is the author of *Postcolonial Love Poem*, winner of the Pulitzer Prize, and *When My Brother Was an Aztec*, winner of an American Book Award. She is a MacArthur fellow and teaches at Arizona State University.

Tarfia Faizullah is the author of *Registers of Illuminated Villages* and *Seam*, winner of a VIDA Award and a GLCA New Writers' Award.

Nick Flynn is the author of several books of poetry, including *Low* and *Some Ether*, which won the PEN/Joyce Osterweil Award, as well as three memoirs, including *Another Bullshit Night in Suck City*.

Katie Ford is the author of several books of poetry, including *If You Have to Go* and *Blood Lyrics*, which was a finalist for the Los Angeles Times Book Prize.

Tess Gallagher is the author of numerous books of poetry, including *Is, Is Not* and *Midnight Lantern: New and Selected Poems*, and several works of fiction, including *The Man from Kinvara: Selected Stories*.

Dobby Gibson is the author of several books of poetry, including *Hold Everything, Little Glass Planet, It Becomes You,* and *Skirmish.*

Christopher Gilbert (1949–2007) was the author of *Across the Mutual Landscape,* which was selected by Michael S. Harper for the Walt Whitman Award of the Academy of American Poets. He is also the author of *Turning into Dwelling,* a posthumous collection of his poetry.

Carmen Giménez is director and publisher of Graywolf Press and the author of six books, including *Be Recorder,* a finalist for the National Book Award, and *Milk and Filth,* a finalist for the National Book Critics Circle Award.

Dana Gioia has published several volumes of poetry, including *Meet Me at the Lighthouse* and *99 Poems: New & Selected,* and numerous critical works, including *Can Poetry Matter?* He has served as chairman of the National Endowment for the Arts and as the California poet laureate.

Leah Naomi Green is the author of *The More Extravagant Feast,* which was selected by Li-Young Lee for the Walt Whitman Award of the Academy of American Poets.

Linda Gregg (1942–2019) was the author of seven books of poetry, including *All of It Singing: New and Selected Poems,* which received the Lenore Marshall Poetry Prize from the Academy of American Poets and the William Carlos Williams Award from the Poetry Society of America.

Jennifer Grotz is the author of several poetry collections, including *Still Falling* and *Window Left Open.* She teaches at the University of Rochester and directs the Bread Loaf Writers' Conferences.

Roy G. Guzmán is the author of *Catrachos.* They have received a fellowship from the National Endowment for the Arts and a Ruth Lilly and Dorothy Sargent Rosenberg Poetry Fellowship.

Marilyn Hacker is the author of numerous books of poetry, including *Presentation Piece*, winner of the National Book Award, as well as many works of translation from the French, including *A House at the Edge of Tears*, *She Says*, and *Nettles* by Vénus Khoury-Ghata.

John Haines (1924–2011) was the author of numerous collections of poems, including *The Owl in the Mask of the Dreamer: Collected Poems*, and the celebrated memoir *The Stars, the Snow, the Fire*.

Saskia Hamilton (1967–2023) was the author of four poetry collections, *As for Dream*, *Divide These*, *Corridor*, and *All Souls*. She was the editor of several volumes of poetry and correspondence, including *The Dolphin Letters, 1970–1979: Elizabeth Hardwick, Robert Lowell, and Their Circle*.

Matthea Harvey is the author of several books of poetry, including *If the Tabloids Are True What Are You?* and *Modern Life*, winner of the Kingsley Tufts Poetry Award.

Fanny Howe is the author of more than thirty works of poetry and prose, including *Love and I*, *The Needle's Eye*, and *Second Childhood*, a finalist for the National Book Award. She was honored with the Griffin Poetry Prize's Lifetime Recognition Award.

Ilya Kaminsky is the author of *Deaf Republic*, winner of the Anisfield-Wolf Book Award and a finalist for the National Book Award, and *Dancing in Odessa*. A finalist for the Neustadt International Prize for Literature, he teaches at Princeton University.

Donika Kelly is the author of *The Renunciations*, winner of the Anisfield-Wolf Book Award, and *Bestiary*, winner of the Cave Canem Poetry Prize, the Hurston/Wright Award, and the Kate Tufts Discovery Award. She teaches at the University of Iowa.

Jane Kenyon (1947–1995) published four collections of poetry and a volume of her translations of Anna Akhmatova. Her posthumous publications include *Collected Poems* and *The Best Poems of Jane Kenyon*.

Vénus Khoury-Ghata is a poet and novelist, the author of the poetry collections *Nettles* and *She Says*, which was a finalist for the National Book Critics Circle Award, and the novel *A House at the Edge of Tears*, all translated from the French by Marilyn Hacker.

Larry Levis (1946–1996) was the award-winning author of five poetry collections, including *Winter Stars* and *The Widening Spell of the Leaves*, and the posthumous collections *Elegy* and *The Darkening Trapeze*.

Liu Xiaobo (1955–2017) received the Nobel Peace Prize in 2010. He was a political activist, poet, and literary critic, and the author of *June Fourth Elegies*, translated from the Chinese by Jeffrey Yang.

Layli Long Soldier is the author of *WHEREAS*, winner of the National Book Critics Circle Award and the PEN/Jean Stein Award, and a finalist for the National Book Award.

Erin Marie Lynch is the author of *Removal Acts*. She is the recipient of a National Endowment for the Arts Fellowship.

Sally Wen Mao is the author of several poetry collections, including *The Kingdom of Surfaces* and *Oculus*, a finalist for the Los Angeles Times Book Prize.

Fred Marchant is the author of several books of poetry, including *Said Not Said*, *The Looking House*, and *Full Moon Boat*. He is an emeritus professor of English at Suffolk University.

Gretchen Marquette is the author of *May Day*, and has published poems in *Harper's*, the *Paris Review*, and *Poetry*.

Jim Moore is the author of many books of poetry, including *Prognosis* and *Underground: New and Selected Poems.*

Harryette Mullen is the author of many books of poetry, including *Urban Tumbleweed, Recyclopedia,* and *Sleeping with the Dictionary,* which was a finalist for the National Book Award, the National Book Critics Circle Award, and the Los Angeles Times Book Prize.

Alice Oswald is the author of many books, including *Falling Awake, Memorial,* and *Spacecraft Voyager 1: New and Selected Poems.* Her poetry has won the Forward Prize, the T. S. Eliot Prize, and the Griffin Poetry Prize.

Don Paterson is the author of numerous books, including *Best Thought, Worst Thought, The White Lie: New and Selected Poetry,* and *Landing Light,* winner of the Whitbread Poetry Award and the T. S. Eliot Prize.

Carl Phillips is the author of many books of poetry, including *Then the War: And Selected Poems 2013–2022,* winner of the Pulitzer Prize; *Pastoral;* and *From the Devotions,* a finalist for the National Book Award. He is also the author of *The Art of Daring: Risk, Restlessness, Imagination* and *Coin of the Realm: Essays on the Life and Art of Poetry.*

A. Poulin, Jr. (1938–1996) was a poet, translator, editor, and the author of many books. He edited and translated *The Complete French Poems of Rainer Maria Rilke.* He founded BOA Editions and directed the press for twenty years.

D. A. Powell is the author of several collections of poetry, including *Useless Landscape, or A Guide for Boys,* which received the National Book Critics Circle Award; *Chronic,* winner of the Kingsley Tufts Poetry Award; and *Repast: Tea, Lunch, and Cocktails.*

Claudia Rankine is the author of *Just Us: An American Conversation; Citizen: An American Lyric*, winner of the National Book Critics Circle Award and the Forward Prize; and *Don't Let Me Be Lonely: An American Lyric*. She is a MacArthur fellow and teaches at New York University.

Rainer Maria Rilke (1875–1926) was an Austrian poet and writer whose works, including *Sonnets to Orpheus* and *Duino Elegies*, are considered classics of twentieth-century literature. Rilke wrote in German and French, and his collected poems in the latter were published as *The Complete French Poems*, translated by A. Poulin, Jr.

Erika L. Sánchez is a poet, essayist, and fiction writer, and the author of *Lessons on Expulsion, Crying in the Bathroom,* and *I Am Not Your Perfect Mexican Daughter*, a finalist for the National Book Award in Young People's Literature.

Claire Schwartz is the author of the poetry collection *Civil Service*. She is a recipient of a Whiting Award and the poetry editor of *Jewish Currents*.

Vijay Seshadri is the author of several collections of poems, including *That Was Now, This Is Then; 3 Sections*, winner of the Pulitzer Prize; and *The Long Meadow*, winner of the James Laughlin Award of the Academy of American Poets.

Diane Seuss is the author of several books of poetry, including *Modern Poetry* and *frank: sonnets*, winner of the Pulitzer Prize, the National Book Critics Circle Award, the Los Angeles Times Book Prize, and the PEN/Voelcker Award.

Solmaz Sharif is the author of *Customs* and *Look*, which was a finalist for the National Book Award. She teaches at the University of California, Berkeley.

Jason Shinder (1955–2008) was the author of *Stupid Hope, Among Women*, and *Every Room We Ever Slept In*, and the editor of *The Poem That Changed America: "Howl" Fifty Years Later.*

Tom Sleigh is the author of many books of poetry, including *The King's Touch; House of Fact, House of Ruin*; and *Space Walk*, winner of the Kingsley Tufts Poetry Award. He is also the author of *The Land between Two Rivers: Writing in an Age of Refugees.*

Danez Smith is the author of several works of poetry including *Bluff, Homie*, a finalist for the National Book Critics Circle Award, and *Don't Call Us Dead*, winner of the Forward Prize for Best Collection and a finalist for the National Book Award.

Tracy K. Smith is the author of several books of poetry, including *Such Color: New and Selected Poems; Wade in the Water*, winner of the Anisfield-Wolf Book Award; and *Life on Mars*, winner of the Pulitzer Prize. She is cotranslator of *My Name Will Grow Wide Like a Tree* by Yi Lei. Smith served as the twenty-second poet laureate of the United States and teaches at Harvard University.

William Stafford (1914–1993) was the author of more than sixty books, including *Traveling through the Dark*, winner of the National Book Award, and *The Way It Is: New and Selected Poems*. He was appointed consultant in poetry to the Library of Congress, and he was named Oregon poet laureate.

Susan Stewart is the author of six books of poetry, including *Cinder: New and Selected Poems* and *Columbarium*, winner of the National Book Critics Circle Award. A former MacArthur fellow and chancellor of the Academy of American Poets, she teaches at Princeton University.

Mary Szybist is the author of *Incarnadine*, winner of the National Book Award, and *Granted*, a finalist for the National Book Critics Circle Award. She teaches at Lewis & Clark College.

Malcolm Tariq is the author of *Heed the Hollow*, which received the Cave Canem Poetry Prize, and *Extended Play*, winner of the 2017 Gertrude Press Poetry Chapbook Contest.

Courtney Faye Taylor is a visual artist and the author of *Concentrate*, which received the Cave Canem Poetry Prize and won the Four Quartets Prize.

Tomas Tranströmer (1931–2015) received the Nobel Prize in Literature in 2011. He was the author of many books of poetry, including *The Half-Finished Heaven: Selected Poems*, translated from the Swedish by Robert Bly. *Airmail: The Letters of Robert Bly and Tomas Tranströmer* collects their correspondence.

Natasha Trethewey is the author of several poetry collections including *Native Guard*, winner of the Pulitzer Prize, *Bellocq's Ophelia*, and *Domestic Work*, winner of the Cave Canem Poetry Prize. She served as the nineteenth poet laureate of the United States.

Mai Der Vang is the author of *Yellow Rain*, a finalist for the Pulitzer Prize, and *Afterland*, winner of the Walt Whitman Award of the Academy of American Poets and longlisted for the National Book Award.

James L. White (1936–1981) was the author of four books of poetry, including *The Salt Ecstasies*, and the editor of two collections of contemporary Native American writing.

Mark Wunderlich is the author of *God of Nothingness*; *The Earth Avails*, winner of the Rilke Prize; *Voluntary Servitude*; and *The Anchorage*, winner of the Lambda Literary Award.

Jenny Xie is the author of *The Rupture Tense*, a finalist for the National Book Award, and *Eye Level*, winner of the Walt Whitman Award of the Academy of American Poets and a finalist for the National Book Award.

Jeffrey Yang is the author of several books of poetry, including *Line and Light*; *Hey, Marfa*; and *An Aquarium*, winner of the PEN/Joyce Osterweil Award. He is the translator of Nobel Peace Prize recipient Liu Xiaobo's *June Fourth Elegies*. Yang is an editor for New Directions.

Yi Lei (1951–2018) published eight collections of poems in her lifetime, as well as *My Name Will Grow Wide Like a Tree*, translated by Tracy K. Smith and Changtai Bi. A recipient of the Zhuang Zhongwen Literature Prize, Yi Lei was one of the most influential figures of Chinese poetry in the 1980s.

Monica Youn is the author of *From From* and three previous poetry collections, including *Blackacre*, a finalist for the National Book Critics Circle Award, and *Ignatz*, a finalist for the National Book Award.

The text of *Raised by Wolves* is set in Arno Pro.
Book design by Rachel Holscher.
Composition by Bookmobile Design & Digital
Publisher Services, Minneapolis, Minnesota.
Manufactured by Friesens on acid-free,
100 percent postconsumer wastepaper.